Recomm

WAYSIDE INNS
OF BRITAIN
1995

A Selection of Hostelries of Character
for Food and Drink and in most cases,
Accommodation

with

Golden Bowl Supplement
for Pet-Friendly Pubs

FHG PUBLICATIONS

Other FHG Publications 1995

Recommended Country Hotels of Britain
Recommended Short-Break Holidays in Britain
Pets Welcome!
Bed and Breakfast in Britain
The Golf Guide: Where to Play/Where to Stay
Farm Holiday Guide England/Wales
Farm Holiday Guide Scotland
Self-Catering & Furnished Holidays
Britain's Best Holidays
Guide to Caravan and Camping Holidays
Bed and Breakfast Stops
Children Welcome! Family Holiday Guide

1995 Edition
ISBN 1 85055 189 8
© FHG Publications Ltd.
No part of this publication may be reproduced by any means or
transmitted without the permission of the Publishers.

Cartography by GEO Projects, Reading
Maps are based on Ordnance Survey maps with the permission of
the Controller of Her Majesty's Stationery Office. Crown copyright reserved.

Typeset by RD Composition Ltd., Glasgow.
Printed and bound in Great Britain by Richard Clay & Co., Bungay, Suffolk.

Distribution. **Book Trade:** WLM, 117 The Hollow, Littleover, Derby DE3 7BS (Tel: 0332 272020.
Fax: 0332 774287).
News Trade: United Magazine Distribution Ltd, 16-28 Tabernacle Street, London EC2A 4BN
(Tel: 0171-638 4666. Fax: 0171-638 4665).

Published by FHG Publications Ltd.
Abbey Mill Business Centre, Seedhill, Paisley PA1 1TJ (0141-887 0428 Fax: 0141-889 7204).
A member of the U.N. Group.

Cover design: Edward Carden (Glasgow)
Cover picture: The Masons Arms at Branscombe, Devon.

———

US ISBN 1-55650-661-9
Distributed in the United States by
Hunter Publishing Inc., 300 Raritan Center Parkway, CN94,
Edison, N.J., 08818, USA

Recommended
WAYSIDE INNS
OF BRITAIN 1995

It's an interesting thought that the origins of the traditional inn have more to do with religion than with the more worldly pleasures with which they are associated in modern times. As you will see from our editorial feature on Beer and Brewing, the earliest inns were established to offer overnight shelter and sustenance to pilgrims. The number and nature of the recipients of this 'holy' hospitality grew and widened over the centuries as the 'public' house which we now know today developed. However, our pubs, inns and small hotels remain a popular source of hospitality for the traveller – as well as the local resident – and we are pleased to offer our latest selection in the 1995 edition of *RECOMMENDED WAYSIDE INNS OF BRITAIN*.

A taste for good beer is certainly not a pre-condition, much less a necessary characteristic of the *WAYSIDE INNS* reader – but it may be of assistance! The continuing existence of a generous range of independent small brewers as well as inn-keepers, is to be encouraged, and the diversity of their products is only one of the many advantages. 'Cheers' to the Independent Family Brewers, and our thanks for their editorial contribution. Our thanks also to Beta Petfoods for the second year of their "Golden Bowl" Award Scheme which aims to recognise pubs and inns which give pets extra consideration. Dogs and cats as well are regular travelling companions, whether simply out walking or on longer journeys. Our **Pet-Friendly Pubs Supplement** includes details of over 100 pet-friendly pubs, nominated for the Golden Bowl Award. We hope this will once again be a useful addition to *RECOMMENDED WAYSIDE INNS*.

Our selection of pubs, inns and small hotels is 'recommended' on the basis of reputation, written descriptions, facilities and long association rather than through personal inspection. We cannot accept responsibility for errors, misrepresentations or the quality of hospitality but we are always interested to hear from readers about their own experiences. Fortunately complaints are few, and rarely serious, but if you do have a problem which cannot be settled on the spot (the best solution, by the way), please let us know. We cannot act as intermediaries or arbiters but we will record your complaint and follow it up with the establishment.

As far as we can establish, the details for all our entries are accurate as we go to press. We suggest, however, that you confirm prices and other specific points at the same time as you are making an enquiry or booking – and we would be grateful if you would also mention *RECOMMENDED WAYSIDE INNS*.

Peter Stanley Williams
Editorial Consultant

Peter Clark
Editorial Director

The Rose and Crown Inn

Mayfield, East Sussex TN20 6TE
Tel and Fax: 01435 872200

Luxury period bedrooms with ensuite bathrooms
Central heating, colour TV, radio alarm, hairdryer
Tea & coffee making facilities, trouser press
Informal candlelit restaurant with excellent wines

This famous Inn sits on the village green of the historic picturesque village
of Mayfield. Dating back to 1546 its unspoilt oak beamed bars with log
fires serve excellent Real Ales and quality bar meals, or you may choose to
dine in the informal candlelit restaurant serving award winning food.

AA QQQQ *Selected & Food Rosette*

E.T.B. 🌷🌷🌷 *Commended*

Good Hotel Guide

Good Food Guide

Egon Ronay

Good Pub Guide

CONTENTS
Recommended
Wayside Inns
OF BRITAIN

ENGLAND

Britain's Best Tradition

WHEREVER you may be in Britain there is one thing you can always be sure of – you're never far from a pub. Traditional pubs and inns, like many in this guide have been an integral part of the British way of life for centuries, and brewing in this country has been traced back to before the Romans arrived.

Beer was originally brewed at home, but brewing as an industry finds its roots in the monasteries, where monks brewed ales for the many travellers and pilgrims who took advantage of their hospitality. As pilgrimages increased, so the monks increased their facilities by adding hostels to accommodate their guests. These hostels were the forerunners of traditional wayside inns. From these early beginnings pubs and beers grew in popularity and became more important to Britain's economy and culture. Tax on beer was introduced by Henry II in the twelfth century, and has been with us in some form or other ever since. As the brewing industry contined to grow, the social stature of brewers also improved.

In 1840 there were almost 50,000 brewers in the UK, many of them small innkeeper brewers producing ale to be sold in the immediate vicinity. However, some brewers had become influential community leaders and powerful business men, often having interests in politics and other businesses associated with brewing and agriculture. By 1900 the number of brewers had fallen to about 6,500 as pubs moved from brewing their own beers to selling

products from larger brewers. Today there are only 100 breweries remaining, with a further 200 pub and micro-breweries.

In addition to beer production, most of these breweries also operate their own estate of pubs. Usually about one third of an estate consists of 'managed' houses and two thirds of the pubs are 'tenanted'. Tenanted houses are where the brewers rent their pubs to licensees and supply them with their products, while licensees are able to run the pub as their own business. Tenanted pubs are an established system which provide mutual benefits to brewers and licensees. A tenancy offers licensees a low-cost entry into running a business with extra benefits such as training, marketing and sales support provided by the brewer, while the brewer has a guaranteed outlet for its beers.

But pubs as we know them are more than just 'beer shops'. Especially in rural areas, pubs are centres for a community's social activities and each pub has its unique characteristics which reflect the identity of the community it serves. Traditional cooking, friendly service and a warm atmosphere are all ingredients which are readily associated with British pubs and which make them the envy of the world. Recent research by the Brewers and Licensed Retailers Association has shown that nine out of 10 Americans visiting the UK prefer British pubs to their own bars. Most Europeans feel the same way, with the French, Italians, Germans, Belgians and Dutch all preferring British pubs.

Pubs are therefore not only vital parts of the British way of life, but also make major contributions to tourism. But why do our pubs fare so much better than continental cafés and bistros? The single largest reason is that their atmosphere is warmer and more homely. A British pub is seen more as a place to relax, meet people and socialise than mere a watering-hole. Of course, this is not to demean the importance of British ales. Traditional British beer is as unique as the pubs which sell them. Cask-conditioned, or 'real', ale is the modern descendent of the brews produced down the centuries, and is still produced to centuries old recipes. The ingredients used in the brewing process – malt (germinated barley), water, hops and yeast – have not changed substantially over the years. Differences between the varied choice of ales are mainly down to closely guarded variations in recipes and the individual techniques used by brewers.

Now modern technology assists traditional brewing techniques so that beautiful old 'coppers' can be seen side by side with pristine new containers. A trip round one of the smaller breweries is a delight to all senses, with a chance to taste the malt and smell the hops, and is an informative journey through history. Growing interest in historical breweries has inspired many to open visitor centres and most offer brewery tours. A number of brewers still employ traditional craftsmen, such as coopers (wooden barrel-makers), and horse-drawn drays can still be seen delivering beer to pubs in some parts of the country.

The vast majority of beer consumed in Britain is now produced by the five largest brewers who supply pubs across the country with well-known brands. It is perhaps the other brewers, however, who contribute more to the cultural traditions of brewing. Smaller regional or local brewers cover most of the country between them, and despite relatively small sales, produce the majority of beer brands available in Britain.

Many of these beers are traditional, cask-conditioned ales, produced by brewers who have often been serving the same pints to the same communities for a century or more. To these brewers their profession is as much an art as a business and care is taken at every step to preserve the quality and traditions which have made their products so popular. 38 such brewers, all independent and family controlled, have joined together to form the Independent Family Brewers of Britain (IFBB), with the aims of preserving the best traditions of British brewing and pubs. Faced with the decline in beer drinking, fierce competition from the national brewers and possible threats to brewers' rights to own their pubs, the future of traditional British brewing may not be as rosy as its past.

All is not lost yet, though. Brewers especially members of the IFBB, are determined to continue providing their much-loved ales, and drinkers are certainly happy to carry on drinking them. Just remember next time you're enjoying a pint whether in your 'local' or visiting one of our Wayside Inns, not only are you sampling one of Britain's best traditions, you're also helping to protect its future.

Recommended
WAYSIDE INNS

ENGLAND

Avon

THE WHEELWRIGHTS ARMS,
Monkton Combe, Near Bath,
Avon BA2 7HD

Tel: 01225 722287

8 bedrooms, all with private shower; Free House with real ale; Historic interest; Bar food; Car park (20); Bath 3 miles.

With excellent accommodation housed in the converted barn and stables, this is a lovely base from which to visit the numerous houses, gardens and places of interest which lie within a few miles, including of course the city of Bath itself. The hostelry stands in the peace and quiet of the lovely Midford valley. A large selection of home cooked food is served, with the addition of a grill menu in the evening. In addition there is a choice of four real ales. The bedrooms (mostly beamed) are equipped with shower, toilet, washbasin, colour television, central heating, tea and coffee making facilities, direct-dial telephones and hairdryers. Terms are very reasonable. The inn is also a lovely base for walking, fishing, riding or just relaxing. In the summer guests are free to use the pleasant garden and patio, and in winter cosy log fires warm the bar.

The **£** symbol when appearing at the end of the italic section of an entry shows the anticipated price, during 1995, for **single full Bed and Breakfast.**

Under £30	**£**	**Over £45 but under £60**	**£££**
Over £30 but under £45	**££**	**Over £60**	**££££**

This is meant as an indication only and does not show prices for Special Breaks, Weekends, etc. Guests are therefore advised to verify all prices on enquiring or booking.

Berkshire

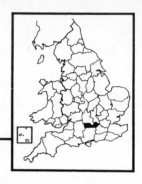

THE YEW TREE,
Andover Road, Highclere, Near Newbury,
Berkshire RG15 9SE
Tel: 01635 253360

6 bedrooms, all with private bathroom; Free House with real ale; Historic interest; Bar and restaurant meals; Car park (40); Winchester 15 miles, Newbury 5; ££££.

The Yew Tree styles itself a "traditional inn, restaurant and rooms", and few who have been fortunate enough to cross its threshold would fail to agree that it fulfils their highest expectations in all departments. Well kept real ales, crackling log fires, and a friendly, informal atmosphere ensure that this 350-year-old hostelry more than lives up to the first part of the description, while comfortable en suite rooms with all modern amenities cater for those who are so enchanted by this delightful area that they wish to linger on. As for the restaurant — here is somewhere really rather special, where the imaginative menus feature only the freshest of produce, and where the thoughtfully selected wine list caters for all tastes and pockets. *Logis of Great Britain, Egon Ronay.*

THE BLACK BOY INN,
Hurley, Maidenhead,
Berkshire SL6 5NQ
Tel: 01628 824212

One bedroom with private bathroom; Brakspear's House with real ale; Historic interest; Bar and restaurant meals; Car park (40); Maidenhead 4 miles; ££.

The "Black Boy" in question was Charles II (so nicknamed because of his swarthy skin), and it is believed that his followers used the building as a safe house while plotting his return. Patrons today are more interested in the extensive bar menu which includes a selection of "pub specials" such as shepherds pie, lasagne, and steak and kidney pie, as well as freshly cut sandwiches, ploughmans and more substantial dishes — not to mention the additional daily "specials" and very moreish puddings. Meals and snacks are served each lunchtime and evening, and diners are sure to find the perfect accompaniment from the wide selection of refreshments available behind the bar. Two cosy bedrooms provide comfortable overnight accommodation.

Buckinghamshire

THE FIVE ARROWS HOTEL,
High Street, Waddesdon,
Buckinghamshire HP18 0JE

Tel: 01296 651727
Fax: 01296 658596

6 bedrooms, all with private bathroom; Free House with real ale; Historic interest; Children welcome; Bar and restaurant meals; Car park; Aylesbury 5 miles; ££££.

Architecturally most striking, the Five Arrows stands at the gates of Waddesdon Manor which was built in the style of a French château at the end of the 19th century by the founder of the Rothschild dynasty. Originally constructed to house the craftsmen and architects working on the Manor, this unique building now offers an opportunity to enjoy wonderful food in a relaxed and informal atmosphere, a choice of real ales including some local brews, and some superb wines, many available by the glass. Healthy appetites are amply catered for here, with the addition at lunchtime of a selection of freshly made sandwiches, ploughmans, and other lighter snacks. Six charmingly appointed en suite bedrooms furnish accommodation for those wishing to explore the many local places of interest. *Egon Ronay "Newcomer of the Year" 1994.*

Cambridgeshire

BRIDGE HOTEL,
Clayhithe, Near Waterbeach,
Cambridgeshire CB5 9NZ

Tel: 01223 860252
Fax: 01223 440448

26 bedrooms, all with private bathroom; Free House with real ale; Historic interest; Children welcome; Restaurant meals; Car park (100); Cambridge 4 miles; £££.

The historic Bridge Hotel is not only one of the most popular luncheon and dinner rendezvous in the area but is internationally famous as a riverside hotel. Situated beside the River Cam just four miles north of Cambridge, the hotel can be easily reached by road or rail. Our riverside restaurant offers you service and individual attention and a full à la carte menu is always available. The Bridge Hotel is fully licensed, and can cater for all kinds of business and private functions. 🌷 🌷 🌷

THE EATON OAK,
Cross Hall Road, Eaton Ford, St. Neots, Cambridgeshire PE19 4AH

Tel: 01480 219555
Fax: 01480 407520

9 bedrooms, all with private bathroom; Charles Wells House with real ale; Children welcome; Bar and restaurant meals; Car park (50); Bedford 11 miles, Huntingdon 9; £££.

Just a moment from the A1, this Georgian-style inn is the ideal place for the family to stop for excellent and reasonably-priced meals in the Charterhouse Restaurant which is open seven days a week. Children are most welcome to dine with their parents and have their own menu. As an alternative, hot and cold bar snacks are served in the lounge and Charles Wells' real ale is a recommended tipple. Grenville and Pauline are your friendly hosts and visitors lured by the conviviality of the house may be tempted to stay overnight: a wise decision for the accommodation is first-class, all guest rooms having en suite facilities with colour television, telephone and tea and coffee-makers.

LEEDS ARMS,
2 The Green, Eltisley, Cambridgeshire PE19 4TG

Tel: 01480 880283
Fax: 01480 880379

9 motel rooms, all with private bathroom; Free House with real ale; Bar food; Car park (40); Cambridge 10 miles, St. Neots 6; £££.

Long before community centres were thought of, the village hostelry was the place to hear all the news, and a lovely old inn like the Leeds Arms is still the hub of local social life, and well deserves to be. Attractively decorated yet still retaining the old oak beams and an inglenook fireplace with copper hood over a blazing log fire to bring a touch of the old days to modern times, the Leeds Arms offers a range of meals to suit all tastes. There is an extensive bar menu with appetisers, succulent steaks and delicious desserts available all week; also Sunday lunch. Accommodation is of an equally high standard, and rooms are well equipped with colour television, telephone and drinks making facilities. *ETB "Listed".*

NOTE

All the information in this book is given in good faith in the belief that it is correct. However, the publishers cannot guarantee the facts given in these pages, neither are they responsible for changes in policy, ownership or terms that may take place after the date of going to press. Readers should always satisfy themselves that the facilities they require are available and that the terms, if quoted, still apply.

THE CROWN AND PUNCHBOWL INN,
Horningsea,
Cambridgeshire CB5 9JG

Tel: 01223 860643
Fax: 01223 441814

5 bedrooms, all with private bathroom; Free House with real ale; Historic interest; Bar meals, restaurant evenings only; Car park; Cambridge 4 miles; ££.

This charming, recently restored 17th century inn, situated in the centre of the unspoilt riverside village of Horningsea which lies four miles north east of Cambridge, is an ideal stopover, not only for visitors to the City but also for those touring East Anglia. In the old bars, with their exposed timbers and inglenook fireplace, open fires throughout the winter months add to the warm welcome provided by the proprietors. The inn is gaining an enviable reputation for its food, which, while quintessentially English, provides original dishes with a menu changing daily. A speciality of the house is a five-course dinner included in the daily and weekend rates. The bedrooms all offer the highest standards of comfort with private bathrooms, tea and coffee making facilities and telephones. Colour televisions are also available.

THE BELL INN HOTEL,
Great North Road, Stilton,
Cambridgeshire PE7 3RA

Tel: 01733 241066
Fax: 01733 245173

19 bedrooms, all with private bathroom; Free House with real ale; Historic interest; Bar and restaurant meals; Car park; Peterborough 6 miles; ££££.

The Bell Inn Hotel, birthplace of Stilton Cheese, is a magnificent old coaching inn, dating back to the 15th century. Built around an old stone courtyard are 19 luxury en suite bedrooms, all offering tea and coffee making, colour television with satellite, hairdryers, and direct-dial telephones; four-poster and de luxe rooms available. The Bell offers old world charm, relaxing comfort and the most modern facilities. Situated on the first floor is a romantic open-vaulted galleried restaurant serving superb food and fine wines. Or if you prefer, we can offer you a popular village bar serving real ale and traditional bar snack meals. 🏨🏨🏨🏨 *Highly Commended, AA ***, Egon Ronay.*

Cheshire

LION AND SWAN HOTEL,
Swan Bank, Congleton,
Cheshire CW12 1JR

Tel: 01260 273115
Fax: 01260 299270

21 bedrooms, all with private bathroom; Courage House with real ale; Historic interest; Bar and restaurant meals; Car park (50); Stoke-on-Trent 11 miles; ££££.

In this fertile land of crumbly cheese, canals, cows and cats that smile and slowly disappear, the worthy Lion and Swan claims to have hosted and victualled travellers from archbishops to executioners since 1496. The hotel has been magnificently restored in all its Tudor glory, yet behind its handsome, black and white timbered facade are contemporary appointments of the highest calibre. Luxury bedrooms and suites feature bathrooms en suite, remote-control colour television, direct-dial telephone and tea and coffee-makers. There are two delightful bars and dining here is a memorable experience, exciting English and Continental dishes gracing the lovely Tudor Rose Restaurant where beams, wood carvings and intriguing antiques make a perfect setting for a perfect meal. *ETB* 🛡 🛡 🛡 🛡 *Commended, RAC and AA ****.

SMOKER INN,
Plumley, Knutsford,
Cheshire WA16 0TY

Tel: 01565 722338

No accommodation; Robinson House with real ale; Historic interest; Children welcome; Bar and restaurant meals; Car park (120); Knutsford 3 miles.

This famous fifteenth century inn (named after a horse!) is situated on the A556 between Manchester and Chester, and those tired of motorway food need only travel two and a half miles from Junction 19 of the M6 to find altogether more appetising sustenance. Meals and snacks are available at lunchtimes and in the evenings, and the extensive menu includes traditional favourites such as steaks, liver and onions, fresh fish and curry, as well as more exotic dishes. Lighter appetites are well catered for with good home-made soup and freshly cut sandwiches. Friendly service, combined with real ales, a fine selection of malt whiskies, comfortable furnishings and a relaxed atmosphere make this an inn definitely well worth seeking out.

THE PHEASANT INN,
Higher Burwardsley, Tattenhall,
Cheshire CH3 9PF
Tel: 01829 70434

8 bedrooms, all with private bathroom; Free House with real ale; Historic interest; Bar and restaurant meals; Car park (60); Chester 9 miles.

For 300 years the lovely half timbered and sandstone Pheasant Inn has stood atop the Peckforton Hills, gazing out over the Cheshire Plain to distant Wales. Panoramic views are to be enjoyed from most of the nicely decorated bedrooms, which are complete with en suite bathroom, colour television, radio alarm, hairdryer and beverage making facilities. Accommodation is in the beautifully converted barn, tucked quietly away from the convivial bar with its huge log fire, and the Bistro Restaurant which enjoys a well-deserved reputation for fine fare, well presented and served with cheerful efficiency. Weekend mini-breaks are a popular feature of this commendable establishment.

Cornwall

HARBOUR LIGHTS HOTEL,
Polkirt Hill, Mevagissey,
Cornwall PL26 6UR
Tel: 01726 843249

7 bedrooms, 5 with private bathroom; Free House with real ale; Bar food; Car park; St Austell 5 miles; ££.

With panoramic views over the harbour of the working fishing village of Mevagissey from its elevated position, this modern, family-run free house is a romantic place to visit. Quite possibly, one may be tempted to stay, for the Bed and Breakfast accommodation is of a high order, most rooms having a far-reaching vista of St. Austell Bay and being blessed with en suite facilities; all have colour television, radio, telephone, hot and cold running water and tea and coffee-makers. There is an extensive bar food menu served every lunchtime and summer evenings. Residents' meals may be taken either in the informal atmosphere of the public bar or in their own no smoking dining room. *Les Routiers.*

OLD FERRY INN,
Bodinnick-by-Fowey,
Cornwall PL23 1LX

Tel: 01726 870237

12 bedrooms, 8 with private bathroom; Free House with real ale; Historic interest; Children welcome; Bar food, restaurant evenings only; Car park (8); Liskeard 15 miles, Looe 10; £££/££££.

Under the supervision of Royce and Patricia Smith, this 400-year-old hostelry, fully licensed, combines the charm of a past era with modern comfort. Rooms are well-appointed, and several bedrooms have private bathrooms. A reputation has been rapidly gained for fine food and wine. This free house stands in a quiet sheltered position facing south, overlooking the beautiful Fowey estuary. Bodinnick is a splendid centre for sailing, boating and fishing; Fowey, easily reached by car ferry, has a famous yachting harbour. There are lovely coastal walks in the vicinity. *British Tourist Authority Commended Country Hotel.*

PORT GAVERNE HOTEL,
Near Port Isaac,
Cornwall PL29 3SQ

Tel: 01208 880244

19 bedrooms, all with private bathroom; Free House with real ale; Historic interest; Bar food, restaurant evenings only; Car park (25); Wadebridge 5 miles; ££££.

Cheerfully efficient service, informality, and wonderfully fresh food combine with cosy and tasteful accommodation to ensure that guests will return again and again to this pretty 17th century inn. All bedrooms have private facilities and are well furnished in a pleasing style; a television room is available in addition to the residents' lounge and two bars. The excellent table d'hôte menu changes daily, although of course guests may dine à la carte if they prefer. Tasty bar snacks are also served in the evening, and packed lunches are available if required. Golfers will be interested in the special breaks which include rounds on the first-class local courses. ❀ ❀ ❀ ❀ *Commended, AA Rosette for Food.*

The Cornish Arms

THE CORNISH ARMS,
Pendogett, Port Isaac,
Cornwall PL30 3HH

Tel: 01208 880263
Fax: 01208 880335

7 bedrooms, 5 with private bathroom; Free House with real ales; Historic interest; Children welcome; Bar and restaurant meals; Wadebridge 8 miles, Polzeath 6, Port Isaac 1.

A delightful 16th century Coaching Inn in the small rural village of Pendogett, just one mile from the coast. Anyone who makes The Cornish Arms a base for exploring the area will not be disappointed by the attractive accommodation or the warmth of welcome extended. Whilst retaining the character of a traditional coaching inn, The Cornish Arms offers all modern amenities in every bedroom; colour and satellite TV, telephone, trouser press, tea and coffee making facilities, etc. The highly recommended restaurant specialises in locally caught seafood and an extensive range of other dishes. Complement your meal with wine from the extensive cellars of The Cornish Arms. Pendogett Special Bitter is famous for its strength — the locals won't touch it, it's so strong. With Bass straight from the barrel, together with other real ales, you will see why both CAMRA and The Good Pub Guide recommend The Cornish Arms. *ETB* 🌺 🌺 🌺 *Commended, RAC**, Les Routiers, Good Food Guide.*

THE HARBOUR INN,
Porthleven, Near Helston,
Cornwall TR13 9JB

Tel: 01326 573876

10 bedrooms, 8 with private bathroom; St. Austell House with real ale; Historic interest; Bar lunches, restaurant evenings only; Car park (15); Helston 2 miles; ££/£££.

Retaining the friendly atmosphere of a typical Cornish fisherman's pub, the Harbour Inn is a much loved part of Porthleven's busy life which is set around the constant ebb and flow of craft in its picturesque harbour. The main bar is a focal meeting point where songs and talk of the sea and ships are commonplace. In addition, the inn has a comfortable lounge bar and a restaurant where a wide range of wines and an extensive range of food from a quality à la carte menu is always available. Fine sands stretch away eastwards from the harbour and at one point form a natural barrier between the sea and freshwater Loe Pool, whilst to the west, the super beach of Praa Sands is ideal for children. Seduced by that sniff of salt in the air? Then just consider the first-rate accommodation to be had at this convivial hostelry. Most rooms have en suite facilities and harbour views and all have colour television, telephone, tea and coffee-makers and hair dryers. Apart from a variety of daily tourist attractions, sporting activities that may be enjoyed locally include boating in all its forms, horse riding, sea and freshwater fishing, surfing, tennis, bowls, golf (nearest course Praa Sands) and walking the Cornish Coastal Path which encompasses the entire county. 🌺 🌺 🌺 *Commended, AA **, Egon Ronay.*

RISING SUN INN,
Portmellon Cove, Mevagissey,
Cornwall PL26 6PL
Tel: 01726 843235

5 bedrooms, all with private shower; Free House with real ale; Children welcome; Bar meals, restaurant evenings only; Car park (60); St Austell 5 miles; £/££.

All Cornish fishing villages nurture a quaint quayside inn or two as part of the scenery. Overlooking Portmellon Cove and within easy walking distance of Mevagissey, the 17th century Rising Sun is no exception to the rule although, perhaps, it is more kempt than quaint. It certainly has impressive modern appointments and is well-known for its wide-ranging lunchtime and evening à la carte menus. A number of attractive coastal and valley walks emanate from this charming little place and it is a good touring centre for exploring the Duchy. There are two friendly bars, highly popular in the summer months, and first-rate accommodation is available, all bedrooms having a shower en suite, colour television and tea and coffee-making facilities. 🐦

DRIFTWOOD SPARS HOTEL,
Trevaunance Cove, St Agnes,
Cornwall TR5 0RT
Tel: 0187-255 2428/3323

10 rooms, all with private facilities; Free House with real ale; Historic interest; Children welcome; Bar and restaurant meals; Large car park; Newquay 12 miles, Truro 8, Redruth 7; ££.

Situated only a hundred yards from the beach, the building which is now the popular Driftwood Spars Hotel is over 300 years old and has seen active service as a tin miners' store, a chandlery, a sailmaker's workshop and a fish cellar. But nowadays the emphasis is strictly on providing guests with good food, ale and atmosphere. There are three bars — one has a children's room — serving a selection of real ales, including a weekly guest beer, and appetising home-cooked food. Delicious candlelit dinners, featuring fresh local seafood, game and steaks, can be enjoyed in the restaurant. Driftwood Spars offers ten bedrooms, all with private facilities, colour television, telephone, tea-making equipment and sea views. Please telephone or write for brochure.

THE RISING SUN,
The Square, St Mawes, Cornwall TR2 5DJ
Tel: 01326 270233

11 bedrooms, 10 with private bathroom; St Austell House with real ale; Children welcome; Bar food, restaurant evenings only; Car park (3); Tregony 10 miles; ££/£££.

Regular patrons of this friendly establishment in the centre of St Mawes make a beeline for the window seats, for they know that from here they get the best (and most comfortable) view of the ever-changing panorama of harbour and waterfront. The light and airy conservatory lounge provides an equally good vantage point, as do those of the pleasantly decorated en suite bedrooms which look to the front. The inn's location on the unspoiled Roseland Peninsula makes it extremely popular with sailors and walkers, who know that they will find here a warm welcome, lively conversation, good food and a first-rate choice of beers, wines and spirits, which in fine weather can be enjoyed in the neat courtyard. *AA***, *Egon Ronay, Johansens, Good Food Guide.*

MOLESWORTH ARMS HOTEL,
Wadebridge,
Cornwall PL27 7DP

Tel: 01208 812055
Fax: 01208 814254

16 bedrooms, 14 with private bathroom; Free House with real ale; Children welcome; Bar food, restaurant evenings only; Car park (20); Bodmin 6 miles; ££.

Cars have now replaced the coaches and carriages that once clattered across the cobbled courtyard of this 16th century coaching inn. Rich panelling, beamed ceilings, cheerful log fires and traditional Cornish hospitality are reminders of those days, although the splendid facilities now to be found at this welcoming hostelry would be well beyond the ken of guests of former years. Under the kind supervision of hosts, Nigel and Shelley Cassidy, the inn is elegantly furnished; two bars invariably buzz with amiable conversation, some guests no doubt studying the comprehensive selection of bar meals. For formal dining, the Coach House Restaurant is justly popular, especially for its fresh local seafood. Excellently appointed overnight accommodation is available. *AA**, Les Routiers.*

Cumbria

ROYAL OAK INN,
Bongate, Appleby-in-Westmorland,
Cumbria CA16 6UN

Tel: 017683 51463
Fax: 017683 52300

9 bedrooms, all with private bathroom; Free House with real ale; Historic interest; Children welcome; Bar and restaurant meals; Car park; Kendal 24 miles, Penrith 13; ££.

Quietly situated in the oldest part of this historic town, the Royal Oak has welcomed guests since the seventeenth century. Colin and Hilary Cheyne ensure that all who enter its portals are met with a friendly welcome and efficient service. Bedrooms are comfortably furnished, with a full range of amenities. One is assured of finding something to suit one's taste (and pocket!) from the well-balanced menu which includes local specialities and more exotic dishes. A range of malt whiskies and hand-pumped real ales can be sampled in the cosy bar. ❀ ❀ ❀ *Highly Commended, AA/RAC**, Johansens, Logis.*

THE BURNMOOR INN,
Boot, Eskdale,
Cumbria CA19 1TG

Tel and Fax: 019467 23224

8 bedrooms, 6 with private bathroom; Free House with real ale; Historic interest; Children welcome; Bar food, restaurant evenings only; Car park (30); Ravenglass 6 miles; ££.

Those searching out the unspoiled charm of the Lakes will not be disappointed in this fine old inn in the ancient village of Boot, nestling among the hills at the foot of Scafell. Lakeland hospitality is legendary, and hosts Tony and Heidi Foster are proud upholders of this tradition, offering excellent food (both in the restaurant and the bar), fine wines and a selection of good ales. Comfortable, cosy en suite twin and double bedrooms make this a perfect base for walkers, climbers and ramblers all year round. Very competitive room rates make an "Escape to Eskdale" a most appealing prospect.

WHEATSHEAF HOTEL,
Beetham, Near Milnthorpe,
Cumbria LA7 7AL
Tel: 015395 62123

6 bedrooms, all with private bathroom; Free House with real ale; Historic interest; Bar and restaurant meals; Car park (35); Carnforth 6 miles; £££.

Off the beaten tourist track in the charming village of Beetham, this most welcoming hostelry is a splendid touring base for excursions to the Lakes and Yorkshire Dales as well as the seaside at beautiful Morecambe Bay. First-rate overnight accommodation is available, each of the comfortable double bedrooms having en suite facilities, colour television and tea and coffee-makers. Tasty bar snacks are served daily at lunchtime and in the evening, whilst the meals dispensed in the attractive dining room are of high quality. Only 100 yards from the main A6 road and 4 miles from Junction 35 of the M6, this is a tranquil and happily placed holiday venue well worth considering. *AA/RAC *.*

WHITE HART INN,
Bouth, Near Newby Bridge,
Cumbria LA12 8JB
Tel: 01229 861229

4 bedrooms, 1 with private bathroom; Free House with real ale; Bar and restaurant meals; Car park (50); Greenodd 2 miles; ££.

This traditional and charming old coaching inn dates from the 17th century. Whilst retaining the ambience of former days, its recently modernised facilities will be of direct interest to lovers of outdoor pursuits for horse riding, watersports, walking, fishing, shooting, climbing and cycling may all be enjoyed locally. The attractive hostelry lies within the Lake District National Park near to the Grizedale Forest and within easy reach of Lake Windermere, Coniston Water and the Lakeside and Haverthwaite Steam Railway. Good ale and food is served here in a happy, relaxed atmosphere and comfortable Bed and Breakfast accommodation is available at reasonable charge.

HARE AND HOUNDS INN,
Bowland Bridge, Grange-over-Sands,
Cumbria   Tel: 015395 68333 (reception) 015395 68777 (guests)

16 bedroooms, most with private bathroom; Free House with real ale; Historic interest; Bar food; Car park (80); Grange-over-Sands 9 miles, Kendal 8, Windermere 7.

With a tranquil situation in the beautiful Winster Valley and yet conveniently near to the popular pleasures of Windermere, the Hare and Hounds is a delightful residential hostelry with a warm welcome for all. All bedrooms have a telephone, colour television and tea/coffee making facilities, and there is a comfortable residents' lounge. The lounge bar with its oak beams, stone walls and log fires has a typical Lakeland atmosphere, and meals are served at midday and in the evening. There is a beer garden and, isolated by the rolling Cartmel Fells, the inn which dates from 1600 is conveniently placed for numerous beauty spots and places of historic interest. Terms for overnight accommodation represent good value, and special bargain breaks in winter are organised. Access and Visa welcome. *ETB* 🐦 🐦 🐦, *Egon Ronay Recommended.*

COLEDALE INN,
Braithwaite, Near Keswick,
Cumbria CA12 5TN   Tel: 017687 78272

12 bedrooms, all with private shower/WC; Free House with real ale; Children welcome; Bar and restaurant meals; Car park (14); Carlisle 30 miles, Cockermouth 10, Keswick 2; ££.

A friendly, family-run Victorian Inn in a peaceful hillside position above Braithwaite, and ideally situated for touring and walking, with paths to the mountains immediately outside our gardens. All bedrooms are warm and spacious, with en suite shower room and colour television. Children are welcome. Home-cooked meals are served every lunchtime and evening, with a fine selection of inexpensive wines, beers and Coledale XXPS and Yates real cask ale. Open all year except midweek lunches in winter. Tariff and menu sent on request.
🐦 🐦 🐦

THE BLACKSMITH'S ARMS,
Talkin Village, Brampton,
Cumbria CA8 1LE
Tel: 016977 3452

5 bedrooms, all with private bathrooms; Free House; Historic interest; Bar and restaurant meals; Car park (30); Carlisle 9 miles, Brampton 1; ££.

The Blacksmith's Arms offers all the hospitality and comforts of a traditional country inn. Enjoy tasty meals served in the bar lounges, or linger over dinner in the well-appointed restaurant. The inn is personally managed by the proprietors, Pat and Tom Bagshaw, who guarantee the hospitality one would expect from a family concern. Guests are assured of a pleasant and comfortable stay. There are five lovely bedrooms, all en suite and offering every comfort. Peacefully situated in the beautiful village of Talkin, the inn is convenient for the Borders, Hadrian's Wall and the Lake District. There is a good golf course, pony trekking, walking and other country pursuits nearby. *FHG Best Bed and Breakfast Diploma Winners 1989.*

BRIDGE HOTEL,
Buttermere, Cumbria CA13 9UZ
Tel and Fax: 017687 70252

22 bedrooms, all with private bathroom; Free House with real ale; Children welcome; Bar food, restaurant evenings only; Car park (60); Cockermouth 10 miles; £££.

One of the most delightful features of a stay at this welcoming Lakeland hotel is undoubtedly the delicious home-baked afternoon tea which is served free of charge to residents — a gesture typical of the generous and friendly spirit which pervades all aspects of life within its sturdy walls. The walkers, tourists and locals who throng here make for a lively atmosphere in the public bars, where well-kept ales and good, fresh food confirm the hotel's popularity and well-deserved local reputation. Those wishing to explore this loveliest of Lakeland valleys at greater length will find cosy, well-equipped bedrooms and special midweek and Short Breaks rates. Recently constructed self-catering accommodation also available if required. 🏆 🏆 🏆 🏆 *Highly Commended, Les Routiers Corps d'Elite, CAMRA Pub of the Year 1992.*

BRITANNIA INN,
Elterwater, Near Ambleside,
Cumbria LA22 9HP
Tel: 015394 37210
Fax: 015394 37311

13 bedrooms, 7 with private facilities; Free House with real ale; Children welcome; Historic interest; Bar food, restaurant evenings only; Car park (10); Coniston 5, Ambleside 4, Grasmere 3; £££.

This genuine old-world, 400-year-old inn overlooking the village green in the delightful unspoilt village of Elterwater is renowned for its fine food and excellent wine cellar, and is also open to non-residents for dinner in the evening. There are nine double bedrooms, six of which have en suite shower and toilet; three twin-bedded rooms, one of which has shower and toilet; and one single room. All have tea and coffee making facilities, telephone, hair dryer, colour television and central heating. With open fires burning cheerfully in the bars, this lively inn is popular for its bar meals, menu and choice of traditional ales. A warm welcome is assured by the proprietor, David Fry and his staff. Facilities nearby include fishing, sailing, fell walking, pony trekking and hound trails. Closed at Christmas. 🏆 🏆 🏆 *Commended.*

SNOOTY FOX TAVERN,
Main Street, Kirkby Lonsdale,
Cumbria LA6 2AH

Tel: 015242 71308
Fax: 015242 72642

5 bedrooms, all with private bathroom; Free House with real ale; Historic interest; Bar and restaurant meals; Car park (8); Lancaster 14 miles; ££.

For years now Proprietor, Jack Shone, and his seventeenth century coaching inn have consistently tended to the needs of weary travellers. Well-kept beers: Timothy Taylors, Theakstons Best and Hartleys XB seduce all explorers into the timeless ambience of the bar. Bed and breakfast presented in five homely bedrooms ensure that the Fox is more soporific than Snooty! The ambitious menu, prepared by nationally acclaimed chefs, is served all day throughout the inn and has something for everyone, confirming that food is definitely the speciality. Explore both the Lakes and the Dales through the heart of the Snooty Fox.

WHOOP HALL INN,
Burrow with Burrow, Kirkby Lonsdale,
Cumbria LA6 2HP

Tel: 015242 71284
Fax: 015242 72154

16 bedrooms, all with private bathroom; Free House with real ale; Historic interest; Children welcome; Bar and restaurant meals; Car park; M6 (Junction 36) 6 miles; £££.

This 350-year-old inn offers all modern comforts in traditionally furnished en suite bedrooms, most with views down the Lune Valley or over the Barbon Fells. Two four-poster rooms are available, and the Lunesdale Suite has been specifically designed for disabled visitors. The imaginatively converted restaurant provides a fitting venue for highly commended cuisine, with specialities including fresh seafood and game in season. In addition, snacks and sandwiches are available in the friendly bar, along with a selection of traditional hand-pulled beers. Close to the Yorkshire Dales, Whoop Hall is just a short drive from Kendal, the Gateway to the Lake District. 🐾🐾🐾🐾 *Commended, AA and RAC **.*

WILSON ARMS,
Torver, Near Coniston,
Cumbria LA21 8BB

Tel: 015394 41237

6 bedrooms, all with private bathroom; Free House; Bar and restaurant meals; Car park (30); Coniston 2 miles.

This friendly inn is situated in the beautiful Lake District, within easy reach of Coniston Water and the central Lakes. This is an ideal walking area, with miles of unspoilt countryside and many fascinating little villages to explore. The Wilson Arms makes a perfect base at any time of year, with the welcome prospect of a delicious home-cooked meal and a cosy log fire at the end of the day. Fishing and riding are also available in the area. The comfortable rooms have television and tea/coffee making facilities. Special terms for weekend breaks apply during November, December and January, excluding Christmas and New Year.

MANOR HOUSE INN,
Oxen Park, Near Ulverston,
Cumbria LA12 8HG
Tel: 01229 861345

5 bedrooms, 4 with private bathroom; Historic interest; Robinsons and Hartleys House with real ale; Children welcome; Bar and restaurant meals; Car park (30); Greenodd 3 miles; ££.

A country inn as traditional as roast beef and Yorkshire (Cumbrian?) pudding, this popular hostelry, so well run by Kevin and Jenny Pyne, is delightfully set in a small hamlet on the edge of the Grizedale Forest, between the southern shores of Lake Windermere and Coniston Water. For a tranquil Lakeland holiday encompassing the bounties of nature and the bounties of excellent food and accommodation, the Manor House takes some beating for value for money. It is a cheerful place too, with fine cask ales, a sun terrace and pub games to aid relaxation and contentment. Apart from appetising luncheons and dinners, which can be complemented by fine wines, bar meals are served daily. 🍺🍺🍺 *Commended, Egon Ronay.*

QUEEN'S ARMS INN,
Warwick-on-Eden, Carlisle,
Cumbria CA4 8PA
Tel: 01228 560699

8 bedrooms, all with private bathroom; Free House with real ale; Historic interest; Children welcome; Bar food; Car park (40); Carlisle 4 miles; ££.

Situated four miles east of Carlisle and only a few minutes' drive from the M6, the Queen's Arms is an ideal base for exploring Hadrian's Wall, the Scottish Borders, the Lake District and the rolling Cumbrian Fells. All bedrooms are en suite, with television, radio/alarm clocks, central heating and tea/coffee making facilities. An extensive bar snack menu is available. There is a modern adventure playground where children can safely play. Dogs welcome and allowed in bedrooms by arrangement. 1992 tariff still applies in 1995 — prices held again. *Tourist Board Listed, Egon Ronay.*

BAY HORSE INN,
Winton, Near Kirkby Stephen,
Cumbria CA17 4HS
Tel: 017683 71451

3 bedrooms, all with private bathroom; Free House with real ale; Historic interest; Bar food; Car park (6); M6 (Junction 38) 11 miles, Appleby 10, Brough 3, Kirkby Stephen 1; £.

A warm and welcoming little inn situated on the western side of the scenic Cumbrian Pennines, and ideally placed as a stopping-off point on your journey north or south on the nearby M6. Resident proprietors Sheila and Derek Parvin offer the warmest of welcomes to all guests, with the finest of traditional ales, good food and comfortable accommodation. Lying as it does in the picturesque Eden Valley, the Bay Horse is also ideal as a touring base for those wishing to stay longer in this lovely part of the country. Open all year.

Derbyshire

BERESFORD ARMS HOTEL,
Station Road, Ashbourne,
Derbyshire DE6 1AA

Tel: 01335 300035
Fax: 01335 300065

12 bedrooms, all with private bathroom; Free House with real ale; Historic interest; Children welcome; Restaurant meals; Car park (30); Derby 13 miles; ££££.

Situated at the gateway to the Peak District, this family-run hotel is ideal for visiting such places as Alton Towers, Carsington Water and Dovedale, as well as many historic buildings. Built at the turn of the century, it offers a warm welcome in a pleasant environment of olde worlde charm. The comfortable en-suite bedrooms have colour television, direct-dial telephone and tea/coffee making facilities. The hotel has a restaurant and two bars, and there is parking for guests' use.

THE ASHFORD HOTEL,
Church Street, Ashford-in-the-Water, Bakewell,
Derbyshire DE45 1QB

Tel: 01629 812725

7 bedrooms, all with private bathroom; Free House with real ale; Historic interest; Children welcome; Bar food, restaurant evenings only; Car park (50); Bakewell 2 miles; ££££.

In a picturesque location in the heart of the Peak District National Park, this splendid little hotel retains a strong aura of the past which is not surprising for the main part of the building dates back to Napoleonic times. It is decorated in delightful rustic style with original oak beams and open log fires forming an ideal background in which to relax. Skilful refurbishment makes full use of colour co-ordinates, bedrooms all having en suite facilities, colour television, radio, direct-dial telephone and tea and coffee-makers. Two rooms have four-poster beds. Apart from a wide range of bar meals, the standard of the chef-prepared à la carte and table d'hôte cuisine in the restaurant is not only high but inspired. 🍺 🍺 🍺 *Commended, AA, Les Routiers, Egon Ronay, CAMRA.*

THE CASTLE HOTEL,
Maine Road, Castleton,
Derbyshire S32 2WG

Tel: 01433 620578
Fax: 01433 621112

9 bedrooms, all with private bathroom; Bass House with real ale; Historic interest; Children welcome; Bar lunches, restaurant evenings only, plus Sunday lunch; Manchester 28 miles, Sheffield 16, Buxton 10; £££.

A delightful blend of 17th century character and 20th century comforts, the Castle is an ideal base for a relaxing break in the heart of the Peak District National Park. This is just how one imagines the perfect English country inn — low beams, cheerful log fires, friendly conversation and good ales — and the management and staff take great pride in upholding the noble traditions of English hospitality. Food is good and plentiful, and can be enjoyed in the lively public bar or in the tranquil surroundings of the Regency Restaurant. Should accommodation be required, a choice of delightfully furnished bedrooms is available, each en suite and with a full range of amenities. This splendid establishment is within convenient reach of many sporting activities and places of interest. *Egon Ronay.*

YE DERWENT HOTEL,
Main Road, Bamford,
Derbyshire S30 2AY

Tel: 01433 651395

10 bedrooms, 2 with private bathroom; Free House with real ale; Historic interest; Children welcome; Bar and restaurant meals; Car park (40); Hathersage 2 miles.

Proprietors David and Angela Ryan take pride in the friendly, home-from-home atmosphere they have created at this rather nice old inn, well situated in the beautiful Peak District National Park. Good home cooking is one of the primary attractions here, and all food is appealingly presented and served in a cheerful and courteous manner. Packed lunches can be provided for residents off on a day's sightseeing, and the barbecues held in the garden are a popular feature of fine summer weekends. Guest rooms are comfortable and well decorated, and all have beverage making facilities, television and extensive rural views. Some are available en suite. *EMTB* 🐝 🐝*, Les Routiers, CAMRA Recommended, Good Pub Guide.*

YE OLDE CHESHIRE CHEESE,
How Lane, Castleton,
Derbyshire S30 2WJ

Tel: 01433 620330

6 bedrooms, all with private bathroom; Free House with real ale; Historic interest; Bar and restaurant meals; Car park (100); Manchester 17 miles, Sheffield 17.

The "Cheshire Cheese Inn" is a delightful 17th century free house situated in Castleton, Derbyshire — the heart of the Peak District National Park. It is an ideal base for walkers and climbers, with other sporting activities in the area including cycling, golf, swimming, gliding, hang gliding, horse riding and fishing. Castleton itself holds many a treat in store, with its caves and mines, including the world famous "Blue John" mine. There are six pretty bedrooms with colour TV and en suite facilities. Our "Village Fayre" menu is available lunchtimes and evenings, all dishes home cooked in traditional manner — pies, lasagne, chilli etc. Daily specials include roast wild boar, smoked chicken and roast hock. Game menu in winter. No juke box, no pool, no machines, just a traditional 17th century inn. Full Fire Certificate. *Les Routiers.*

THE CHARLES COTTON HOTEL,
Hartington, Near Buxton,
Derbyshire SK17 0AL

Tel: 01298 84229
Fax: 01335 42742

13 bedrooms; Free House with real ale; Historic interest; Children welcome; Bar and restaurant meals; Car park (16); Ashbourne 9 miles; ££££.

The Charles Cotton is a small comfortable hotel with a starred rating for the RAC and AA. The hotel lies in the heart of the Derbyshire Dales, pleasantly situated in the village square of Hartington, with nearby shops catering for all needs. It is renowned throughout the area for its hospitality and good home cooking. Pets and children are welcome; special diets are catered for. The Charles Cotton makes the perfect centre to relax and enjoy the area, whether walking, cycling, pony trekking, brass rubbing or even hang gliding. 🏵🏵🏵

THE GEORGE HOTEL,
Hathersage, Near Sheffield,
Derbyshire S30 1BB

Tel: 01433 650436
Fax: 01433 650099

18 bedrooms, all with private bathroom; Whitbread House with real ale; Historic interest; Children welcome; Bar and restaurant meals; Car park (30); Bakewell 8 miles; ££££.

One of the last havens of unspoiled countryside in this increasingly built-up and built-over land of ours, the Peak District National Park offers a chance to escape from the pressures of the workaday world. Right in the heart is the picturesque village of Hathersage, where the George Hotel offers all that is best in food, refreshment and comfortable accommodation. The traditionally furnished Charlotte Restaurant enjoys an excellent reputation for the high standard of its menus and service, with Sunday roast lunch very popular. Accommodation is of the same high standard, with especially attractive weekend rates to tempt the passing traveller to linger awhile. 🏵🏵🏵🏵, *AA***.*

BARLEY MOW INN,
Main Street, Kirk Ireton, Ashbourne,
Derbyshire DE6 3JP

Tel: 01335 370306

5 bedrooms, all with private bathroom; Free House with real ale; Historic interest; Bar snacks lunchtimes; Car park; Wirksworth 3 miles; £/££.

A village pub in the good old-fashioned, traditional style that is unfortunately fast becoming a rarity, the Barley Mow stands at the top of the main street in this tranquil little village which seems to have been bypassed by much of the noise and clamour of the 20th century. If spending a day walking in the Peak District, inspecting one of the nearby stately homes, or browsing through one of the historic market towns in the area, this is an ideal spot to recharge one's batteries over a delicious locally baked filled roll or perhaps a glass of one of the well kept real ales on offer. Cosy, country-style bedrooms are available should you succumb to the charm of this delightful area.

THE DOG AND PARTRIDGE COUNTRY INN,
Swinscoe, Ashbourne,
Derbyshire DE6 2HS

Tel: 01335 343183
Fax: 01335 342742

29 bedrooms, all with private bathroom; ; Free House; Historic interest; Children welcome; Bar and restaurant meals; Car park (100); Ashbourne 3 miles; ££££.

Mary and Martin Stelfox welcome you to a family-run seventeenth century inn and motel set in five acres, five miles from Alton Towers and close to Dovedale and Ashbourne. We specialise in family breaks, and special diets and vegetarians are catered for. All rooms have private bathrooms, colour television, direct-dial telephone, tea-making facilities and baby listening service. It is ideally situated for touring Stoke Potteries, Derbyshire Dales and Staffordshire moorlands. The restaurant is open all day, and non-residents are welcome. 🏵🏵🏵🏵

GEORGE HOTEL,
Tideswell,
Derbyshire

Tel: 01298 871382
Fax: 01298 872408

4 bedrooms; Historic interest; Bar and restaurant meals; Car park (30); Chatsworth 10 miles, Buxton 9, Bakewell 8; ££.

The church of this ancient market town is known as the "Cathedral of the Peak" and visitors come from far and wide to see it. Next door, the George offers tourists to the Peak District hospitality in keeping with its history as an old coaching inn dating from 1730. A four-poster suite is available for honeymoons or other special occasions. All meals are served every day of the week and a wide range of appetising snacks is also obtainable over the bar. Live 60s music every Friday evening. Used in the TV series "Yesterday's Dreams" set in this "best kept" Derbyshire village.

Devon

THE LONDON INN,
Combe Martin,
Devon EX34 0NA

Tel: 01271 883409

9 bedrooms, one with private bathroom; Free House with real ale; Historic interest; Bar food; Car park (50); Ilfracombe 4 miles.

This charming inn is situated just one mile from the sea and the magnificent North Devon coastline, ideally placed for touring the West Country and for activities such as swimming, boating, fishing, golf and riding. Bedrooms have been recently refurbished and there is a new residents' lounge for relaxation and friendly conversation. Home-made dishes feature prominently on the extensive bar menu, and the residents' dining room provides excellent evening meals and a traditional roast on Sundays. Bed and breakfast rates are real value for money, with reductions for children and longer stays.

THE THREE HORSESHOES,
Branscombe, Seaton,
Devon EX12 3BR

Tel: 0129 780251

Accommodation; Real ale; Historic interest; Sidmouth 5 miles.

A lovely 16th century coaching house with log fires and brasses, set in an area of outstanding natural beauty. Central for sea or country; footpaths lead through woodland and cliff walks. Wonderful wildlife in the area. Honiton, which has many antique shops and is noted for lace making, is nearby, as is historic Exeter; Sidmouth is just ten minutes away. All bedrooms are centrally heated and have tea/coffee making facilities. There is "trad" jazz every Saturday night in the function room, and there is a lounge bar for those who want a quiet drink. Jan and John Moore will give you the warmest of welcomes and help you plan your outings if you wish.

THE RED LION INN,
Dittisham, Near Dartmouth,
Devon TQ6 0ES

Tel: 01803 722235
Fax: 01803 722396

5 bedrooms, all with private bathroom; Free House with real ale; Children over 12 years welcome; Bar and restaurant meals; Car park (12); Dartmouth 6 miles; ££.

The Red Lion has been offering generous hospitality since 1750 when it was a Coaching House. Log fires and gleaming brass in a friendly old bar, hearty English breakfasts, terraced gardens overlooking the River Dart, and an exceptionally warm welcome all await you. Bedrooms are individually furnished, with comfortable beds, central heating and tea-making facilities. An extensive menu includes daily specials and features fresh produce, prime local meats, fresh fish and locally grown vegetables. Picturesque countryside and a mild climate make this a perfect holiday retreat. *Guild of Master Caterers.*

Please mention
Recommended WAYSIDE INNS
when seeking refreshment or
accommodation at a Hotel
mentioned in these pages

THE NOBODY INN,
Doddiscombsleigh, Near Exeter,
Devon

Tel: 01647 252394

Fax: 01647 252978

7 bedrooms, 5 with private bathroom; Free House with real ale; Historic interest; Bar food, restaurant Tuesday to Saturday evenings only; Car park; Exeter 7 miles, Dunsford 4; £££.

There is always somebody in the quaintly named Nobody Inn, for it is extremely popular with visitors and locals alike, and the bars thrum constantly with friendly conversation. A typical Devonshire hostelry in typical Devonshire countryside, the inn originated in the sixteenth century as an ale and cider house for miners working nearby. Today it offers more sophisticated facilities, but still in the warm, traditional style. A well-stocked bar with a cheerful log fire offers a variety of over 230 whiskies, including a large selection of malts, and bar snacks are a popular order. Would-be gourmets are recommended to the à la carte restaurant where well-cooked and attractively presented food, supported by 750 fine wines, satisfy the most obdurate palate. The inn specialises in Devon cheeses and there are often 40 varieties on offer. These, plus the wine and the whiskies, are also available by mail order. Real old world charm is epitomised in accommodation which skilfully incorporates the most modern amenities, including showers, without spoiling the effect. The adjoining manor house, Town Barton, offers further accommodation in the Georgian style, although the house dates from the thirteenth century. All the Torbay resorts are within easy reach by car, and the edge of Dartmoor National Park is only half a mile away. Fishing and shooting with tuition if required may be arranged, whilst walkers will find this an ideal base for a variety of rambles.

THE ROYAL OAK INN,
Dunsford, Near Exeter,
Devon EX6 7DA

Tel: 01647 52256

8 bedrooms, 5 with private bathroom; Free House with real ale; Children welcome; Bar food; Car park (40); Exeter 6 miles, Moretonhampstead 4; £/££.

A friendly welcome awaits you in this traditional country inn, situated six miles west of Exeter just off the B3212. Quiet, en suite accommodation is available in a newly converted 300-year-old traditional cob barn in the beautiful thatched village of Dunsford. This is an ideal base for Dartmoor, Exeter and the coast, with outstanding views across the Teign Valley. Home-made meals are served seven days a week at lunchtimes and in the evenings, and there are always six real ales on offer. Well-behaved dogs are welcome. Please contact Alison or Guy Arnold for details. *Tourist Board Listed "Approved", CAMRA, Good Pub Guide.*

THE TALLY HO COUNTRY INN & BREWERY,
Hatherleigh,
Devon EX20 3JN

Tel: 01837 810306

3 bedrooms, all with private bathroom; Free House with real ale; Historic interest; Bar food, restaurant evenings only (not Wed, Thurs or Sun); Car park (5); Okehampton 7 miles; ££.

Real ales brewed on the premises are just one of the reasons for the popularity of this neat little country inn — just try a glass of Pot-boilers Brew or Tarka Tipple if you need convincing! Equally popular with locals and visitors alike is the impressive range of food, with regular evenings devoted to pizzas, barbecues and fish dishes. Bar meals are available each lunchtime and evening, and on Monday, Tuesday, Friday and Saturday evenings diners can choose from an imaginative à la carte menu presented in the cosy restaurant. Spick and span bedrooms provide comfortable overnight accommodation if required; fishing and golf can be arranged locally for the actively inclined.

THE HUNTERS' INN,
Heddon's Mouth, Parrracombe,
Devon EX31 4PY

Tel: 01598 763230

10 bedrooms, 8 with private bathroom; Free House with real ale; Historic interest; Children welcome; Bar and restaurant meals; Car park; Lynton 4 miles.

This unique inn with the "pub-like" atmosphere is situated in one of the most beautiful valleys in North Devon, lying between Lynton and Combe Martin. Wildlife abounds and peacocks roam free. There are many lovely walks, particularly the one-mile walk to the rocky cove at Heddon's Mouth. The inn offers a well-stocked bar with a fine selection of real ales, a Buttery catering for hot or cold meals, and comfortable accommodation. Bedrooms have bathrooms en suite, colour television, hospitality trays and electric blankets; some have four-poster beds. The inn is completely centrally heated, so you can be sure of a welcome as warm as that offered by the resident proprietor and his caring, courteous staff.

CHURCH HOUSE INN,
Holne, Near Ashburton,
Devon TQ13 7SJ

Tel: 013643 208

6 bedrooms, 4 with private bathroom; Free House with real ale; Historic interest; Children welcome; Bar and restaurant meals; Car park (6); Ashburton 3 miles; ££.

Very much the heart of the village in both location and spirit, this family-run inn dates from 1329 and is a Grade II Listed building. Up to twelve guests can be accommodated, and four of the pleasantly furnished, comfortable bedrooms have their own private bathroom. All are provided with tea and coffee facilities and colour television, and residents have the use of an attractive private sitting room where books, magazines and writing materials are available. Wherever possible local produce is used in the freshly prepared dishes served in the bar and in the restaurant, and a nice range of wines, real ale and cider meets all tastes in refreshment. ❦ ❦ ❦ *Commended, Egon Ronay, Good Pub Guide, Good Food Guide, CAMRA.*

JOURNEY'S END INN,
Ringmore, Near Kingsbridge,
Devon

Tel: 01548 810205

4 bedrooms, 2 with private bathroom; Free House with real ale; Historic interest; Bar and restaurant meals; Car park; Plymouth 17 miles, Bigbury 2.

Dating from 1300, the Journey's End was prescribed a New Inn in the reign of Elizabeth I, and R.C. Sherriff wrote part of his play *Journey's End* here. Set in a beautiful and unspoilt thatched village amidst the rolling South Hams countryside, and only 15 minutes from quiet National Trust coast, this hostelry is a haven for the thirsty, hungry or weary traveller. In the oak-panelled bar a wide range of cask-conditioned ales may be supped, and there is an extensive and inviting food menu. The charming cottage-style bedrooms provide an exceptionally high standard of comfort, two with beautifully appointed private bathrooms. There is also a family suite. All rooms have colour television, personal radio, and tea-making facilities. In winter, a blazing log fire provides warmth in the bar, and individually controlled central heating ensures comfort in the bedrooms. This ancient inn is an ideal centre for holidaymaking at all times of the year. Golf, sea and river fishing, numerous coves and unspoilt beaches, the moors, Plymouth and Kingsbridge are all within easy reach.

OLD SAWMILL INN,
Watermouth, Ilfracombe,
Devon EX34 9SX

Tel: 01271 882259

4 bedrooms, all with shower and toilet; Free House with real ale; Historic interest; Children welcome; Bar food, restaurant evenings only (October to April); Car park (48); Barnstaple 10 miles; ££.

Beautifully placed on the rugged North Devon coast between Ilfracombe and Combe Martin, this is both an interesting and convivial hostelry. Built in 1667, it was originally a water-driven sawmill. The stream, which flows through the beer garden, was diverted to the rear of the building where it turned the wheel. Considerably extended since that time, the inn still retains the 'olde-worlde' atmosphere with its original beams, open log fire and stone fireplace and original saw blades on display. Pub food is served every lunchtime and evening, all meals cooked by resident chefs and the bar also offers a selection of real ales. This happy and well-run hostelry fosters traditional pub activities, such as pool, darts and skittles. A group of Morris Dancers comes to dance outside during the summer, and occasionally a folk group plays in the bar for a good old-fashioned sing-along. Excellent en suite accommodation has been introduced above a recent extension. All rooms are furnished in pine and have colour television, hairdryer and tea and coffee-making facilities. Terms for Bed and Breakfast are extremely reasonable. Combining all the pleasures of a scenic seaside holiday with honest-to-goodness entertainment, the Old Sawmill merits the closest consideration.

RISING SUN HOTEL,
Harbourside, Lynmouth,
Devon EX35 6EQ

Tel: 01598 53223
Fax: 01598 53480

16 bedrooms, all with en suite shower/bathroom; Free House; Historic interest; Children over 5 years welcome; Bar and restaurant meals; Barnstaple 20 miles, Minehead 17; £££.

This fourteenth century smugglers' inn overlooking the harbour and river is steeped in history, with oak panelling, crooked ceilings, thick walls, and uneven oak floors. All the bedrooms have recently been refurbished to a very high standard and the roof re-thatched. The excellent restaurant specialises in local game and seafood. It is claimed that R.D. Blackmore wrote part of his novel 'Lorna Doone' whilst staying at The Rising Sun. The poet Shelley spent his honeymoon in 1812 in a cottage, now named after him, which is part of the hotel. It has a four-poster bed and a comfortable sitting room, and is ideal for a special holiday occasion. Guests can relax in the beautifully landscaped garden and free fishing is available on the hotel's private stretch of salmon river. 🌷🌷🌷 *Highly Commended, AA **, RAC ** and Merit Awards, Johansens "Inn of the Year 1991", Egon Ronay, Les Routiers Casserole Award, Good Hotel Guide Recommended, Good Pub Guide.*

THE BULL AND DRAGON,
Meeth, Okehampton,
Devon EX20 3EP

Tel: 01837 810325

No accommodation; Free House with real ale; Historic interest; Children welcome; Bar and restaurant meals; Car park (20); Hatherleigh 3 miles.

It is worth coming a long way to dine here. Our acquaintance with this charming old thatched hostelry was one of our most joyous experiences — once we had found it! Sheepwash, Winkleigh and then Meeth we spotted on the map — such evocative names; sleepy villages so far removed from urban strife. Warm, welcoming and unpretentious, we found the inn on the A386 Torrington – Okehampton road. Quite apart from an extensive bar menu, Hosts, Brian and Sue Gibbs have certainly compiled a mouth-watering and imaginative array of starters, main courses, vegetarian dishes, sweets and ice-cream specialities at remarkably moderate prices. Suitably engorged, we determined that this super little place deserved a high place on our selective West Country list. A gem indeed!

LONDON INN,
Molland, Near South Molton,
Devon EX36 3NG

Tel: 01769 550269

3 bedrooms, all with private bathroom; Free House with real ale; Historic interest; Children welcome; Bar and restaurant meals; Car park; South Molton 6 miles; ££.

In an idyllic setting on the southern fringe of Exmoor, this charming 15th century inn exudes an aura of peace and good fellowship, yet it was not so on one infamous occasion when miners' wives from nearby Simonsbath, angered by their husbands drinking away their pay, descended upon them with overflowing chamber-pots! Today, the cosy old hostelry with its oak beams and wooden settles, is renowned for its superb home cooking, especially the game pie and trout dishes, whilst appetising bar meals are also served. The local hunt and shooting parties still meet at the inn and for a real feel of rural Devon life, a visit is recommended. Comfortable Bed and Breakfast accommodation is available. 🌷🌷🌷

TAW RIVER INN,
Sticklepath, Okehampton,
Devon EX20 2NW
Tel: 01837 840377

4 bedrooms, 2 with private bathroom; Free House with real ale; Historic interest; Bar food; Car park; Okehampton 4 miles; £.

This little thatched inn, run by John and Tania Attewell, is the nearest thing to storybook Devon as we are ever likely to find. Serving a number of real ales and local cider, the friendly, old-world bar also dispenses a variety of tempting meals, including vegetarian dishes. Local produce figures prominently and we must put in a special word for the delicious sausages, supplied, like all the meat, by the village butcher. On the edge of Dartmoor, with views of Cawsand Beacon and Skaigh Woods, this is the answer to the perfect away from it all holiday. Limited but excellent overnight accommodation is available at moderate rates which, incidentally, includes a massive English breakfast. A real gem.

WHITE HART INN,
The Square, Moretonhampstead, Near Newton Abbot,
Devon TQ13 8NF
Tel: 01647 440406; Fax: 01647 440565

20 bedrooms, all with private bathroom; Free House with real ale; Children over 10 years welcome; Bar and restaurant meals; Car park (10); Exeter 11 miles; £££.

Moretonhampstead is the "gateway" to 365 square miles that make up Dartmoor National Park, ideal for walking and relaxing. The White Hart, an historic coaching inn, has stood in the town square for over 350 years. It has 20 de-luxe bedrooms en suite, with colour television, courtesy trays, hairdryers and telephones; bathrooms have power showers, big fluffy towels and complimentary toiletries. Our restaurant is famous for good food (and plenty of it!), using local meat, fresh fish, vegetables, and cream from Devon farms. Bar snacks are served in the cosy lounge and the oak-beamed bar which also has a selection of real ales. "The most famous coaching inn on Dartmoor". 🌷 🌷 🌷 🌷 *Highly Commended, AA and RAC **, Egon Ronay, Logis.*

RING OF BELLS,
North Bovey,
Devon TQ13 8RB
Tel: 01647 40375

3 bedrooms, all with private bathroom; Free House with real ale; Historic interest; Children welcome; Bar food, restaurant evenings only; Car park; Moretonhampstead 2 miles.

Sheltered by the surrounding thatched houses, this 13th century inn sits snugly in the unspoilt moorland village of North Bovey. Dartmoor and its many attractions are within easy reach, and activities such as fishing and pony trekking can be arranged for guests. Local cider and well kept real ales are an ideal accompaniment to the tasty bar food menu, with choices ranging from ploughman's and salads to local trout and pheasant in season. Other attractions include a swimming pool, beer garden and children's play area. En suite bedrooms with four-poster beds are available at rates that prove a definite temptation to linger longer in this charming spot. *Egon Ronay Recommended.*

PLUME OF FEATHERS INN,
Princetown, Yelverton,
Devon PL20 6QG
Tel: 01822 890240

Two bedrooms; Free House with real ale; Historic interest; Children welcome; Bar food; Car park (100); Tavistock 7 miles; £.

Never mind the infamous prison, the splendid Plume of Feathers is a far more cheerful prospect. High on Dartmoor, it is Princetown's oldest building dating from 1785 and has an abundance of character. It also has plenty of vitality as a traditional family-run inn with plenty of facilities for the young. There is live music every Sunday lunchtime and occasionally on Friday nights, of high standard as we can aver. We dined well from an extensive à la carte menu and wished we could have stayed longer. Bed and Breakfast accommodation is available and there is a camping area and excellently appointed dormitories with bunk beds for the various groups of hikers, adventure and school parties who use the hostelry as base camp.

BLUE BALL INN,
Sidford, Near Sidmouth,
Devon EX10 9QL
Tel: 01395 514062

3 bedrooms; Devenish House with real ale; Historic interest; Children welcome; Bar and restaurant meals; Car park; Sidmouth 2 miles; ££.

Thatched and built of cob and flint, the delightful Blue Ball dates back to 1385 and, proving that practice makes perfect, has been run by the Newton family since 1912. Just a mile or so inland, this is a rewarding place to visit — or even stay, for extremely comfortable accommodation is available, residents having their own lounge with colour television. Super bar food is cheerfully served, there being a surprisingly large choice of main meals, salads, snacks and sweets as well as several vegetarian dishes: local fish is a speciality. There are three bars and, parents please note, extensive family dining facilities. Attractive gardens incorporate a barbecue area which comes into its own in the summer months.

TOWER INN,
Slapton, Kingsbridge,
Devon TQ7 2PN

Tel: 01548 580216

3 bedrooms; Free House with real ale; Historic interest; Children welcome; Bar and restaurant meals; Car park; Dartmouth 5 miles; £.

Famed for its selection of real ales, this well-run 14th century hostelry has other reasons to thank for its popularity, quite apart from its admirable refreshment and cheerful service. Its position is both unusual and fortunate for it is happily sandwiched between the three-mile expanse of Slapton Sands and the well-known nature reserve of Slapton Ley, a freshwater lake fringed by woodland and marshes. Furthermore, superb South Hams countryside lies within easy reach in company with many delightful creeks and beaches. There is always an interesting range of dishes on offer in the restaurant, including a vegetarian selection. Bed and breakfast terms offer excellent value. *CAMRA, Good Pub Guide, Egon Ronay.*

TOM COBLEY TAVERN,
Spreyton, Crediton,
Devon EX17 5AL

Tel: 0164-723 1314

2 double rooms, 2 single rooms; Free House with real ale; Historic interest; Children welcome; Bar and restaurant meals; Car park; Okehampton 7 miles; £.

A small country pub in a quiet and unspoilt mid-Devon village and with an interesting history, the Tom Cobley Tavern has had its moments of fame. Thomas Cobley, of Widecombe Fair fame, was born and died in the parish. His grave citing 1844 as the year of his demise may still be seen in the churchyard. It is fair to suppose that the group of bucolic fun-seekers (and the grey mare) gathered at the inn at the start of their ill-fated journey. Spreyton lies just to the north of the Dartmoor National Park and within easy reach of both north and south coasts. Good wholesome accommodation and home-cooked food is available at very moderate rates.

THELBRIDGE CROSS INN,
Thelbridge, Near Witheridge,
Devon EX17 4SQ

Tel and Fax: 01884 860316

8 bedrooms, all with private bathroom; Free House with real ale; Historic interest; Children welcome; Bar food, restaurant evenings only; Car park (40); Chulmleigh 7 miles; ££.

No juke box, no pool table, just utter tranquillity and superb, home-cooked food. These qualities outline the salient attractions of this picturesque country inn run so hospitably by Bill and Ria Ball. Tradition dies hard: this is the only inn left where the original Lorna Doone Stage Coach still calls to enable passengers to savour Ria's outstanding cuisine. The 'No Smoking' restaurant is open seven days a week for dinners and the beamed bar, warmed by log fires in cool weather, is a great place to relax. In the depths of glorious rural mid-Devon, this is a wonderful place to get away from it all with delightful rooms (all en suite) awaiting peace-loving guests. *ETB* 🌷🌷🌷 *Commended, Egon Ronay.*

KING'S ARMS INN,
Stockland, Near Honiton,
Devon EX14 9BS
Tel: 01404 881361/881732

3 bedrooms, all with private bathroom; Free House with real ale; Historic interest; Children welcome; Bar lunches, restaurant evenings only; Car park (40); Axminster 5 miles; ££.

The delights of rural East Devon, a friendly and intimate atmosphere, excellent home cooking and easy access to the coast and many places of interest represent four-square reasons for singling out this recommended hostelry for a visit. The mouth-watering menu is displayed on the blackboard in the Cotley Restaurant and the style of cooking is an appetising blend of the classic, nouvelle and modern, all combining to produce hearty and memorable meals. An attractive place in which to stay, the inn has limited but nonetheless first-rate accommodation, comprising one twin and two double rooms, each with bathroom en suite, television, telephone and tea and coffee-makers.

MERRIEMEADE HOTEL,
Lower Town, Sampford Peverell, Near Tiverton,
Devon EX16 7BJ
Tel: 01884 820270; Fax: 01884 821614

5 bedrooms, all with private bathroom; Free House with real ale; Historic interest; Bar and restaurant meals; Children welcome; Tiverton 5 miles; ££.

Not far from the Grand Western Canal, now resuscitated for leisure purposes, this is the place to visit for English and French cuisine of the very highest order. Chef/Proprietor, Patrick Jean-Pierre, is the culinary magician and his imaginative dishes are accompanied by a wide choice of unusual desserts and wines. The restaurant and bar are open daily for lunches, dinners and bar snacks. Outside is a lovely garden with a pond and children's play area. The hotel is set in unspoilt countryside and those seeking a tranquil holiday base would do well to consider the fine en suite accommodation available here. 🐾🐾🐾 *Commended, Les Routiers.*

THE GLOBE HOTEL,
Topsham, Near Exeter,
Devon EX3 0HR

Tel: 0139-287 3471
Fax: 0139-287 3879

17 bedrooms, all with private bathroom; Free House with real ale; Historic interest; Bar and restaurant meals; Car park (20); Exeter 4 miles; ££.

Dark oak panelling, comfortable leather armchairs and period prints all contribute to the traditional character of this sixteenth century coaching inn which stands on the main street of the ancient town of Topsham, on the estuary of the River Exe. Those seeking overnight accommodation will find comfortable bedrooms, all with private bathrooms, colour television, direct-dial telephone, and tea and coffee making facilities. For an extra touch of luxury, rooms are available with four-poster or half-tester beds. The good value range of bar meals includes all the traditional favourites, and in the restaurant a full à la carte menu is served with courtesy and efficiency. *South West Tourist Board* 🍺 🍺 🍺.

Dorset

THE FOX INN,
Ansty, Near Dorchester,
Dorset

Tel: 01258 880328
Fax: 01258 881097

14 bedrooms, all with private bathroom; Free House with real ale; Historic interest; Children welcome; Bar and restaurant meals; Milton Abbas 2 miles; £££.

Set in remote and beautiful countryside, this noted inn is well known for its excellent food. The cold carvery offers a wide selection of cold meats, pheasant, duckling, sundry pies and many other items depending on the season, and has proved to be extremely popular all year round, with an extensive selection of salads and dressings to accompany the range of meats. In addition a wide variety of bar snacks are offered, together with the ever popular dishes prepared on the indoor barbecue, including succulent steaks, chicken, swordfish, spare ribs etc. The Fox is an extremely interesting venue for lunch or dinner, as not only will you enjoy the food, but you can also admire the huge collection of toby jugs, now over 800 and thought to be the largest in Europe. There is also a large collection of plates in the Platter Bar and Restaurant.

THE SPYWAY INN,
Askerswell, Near Dorchester,
Dorset DT2 9EP
Tel: 01308 485250

No accommodation; Free House with real ale; Bar food; Car park; Bridport 4 miles.

With a well-deserved and ever-growing reputation for excellent real ale and appetising country fare, the attractive and welcoming Spyway is well worth a detour from the busier Dorset resorts. Refreshments to quench every kind of thirst are available, ranging from hand pumped real ales, around 40 different whiskies, and country wines to an intriguing selection of pure Dorset apple juices. Bar food helpings are both reasonably priced and plentiful. The quiet garden has a fish pond and pets' corner and there is plenty of opportunity to stretch one's legs along one of the nearby paths.

ANVIL HOTEL,
Salisbury Road, Pimperne, Blandford,
Dorset DT11 8UQ
Tel: 01258 453431/480182

9 bedrooms, all with private bathroom; Free House; Historic interest; Children welcome; Bar and restaurant meals; Car park (30); Bournemouth 26 miles, Salisbury 24, Poole 16; ££££.

A long, low thatched building set in a tiny village deep in the Dorset countryside — what could be more English? And that is exactly what visitors to the Anvil will find — a typical old English hostelry dating from the sixteenth century, set in an English country garden and offering good old-fashioned English hospitality. A mouthwatering full à la carte menu with delicious desserts is available in the charming beamed and flagged restaurant and a wide selection of bar meals in the attractive, fully licensed bar. All bedrooms have private facilities. Ample parking. Clay pigeon shooting and tuition for individuals. *ETB* 🏵 🏵 🏵 *Commended, RAC and AA**, Good Food Pub Guide, Les Routiers.*

AVON CAUSEWAY HOTEL,
Hurn, Christchurch, Bournemouth,
Dorset BH23 6AS
Tel: 01202 482714
Fax: 01202 477416

14 bedrooms, all with private bathroom; Free House with real ale; Historic interest; Children welcome; Bar and restaurant meals; Car park (200); Bournemouth 5 miles; ££.

A most unusual hotel built around the old Hurn Railway Station on the Southern Line, the Avon Causeway reminds one of its origins with the locomotive and beautifully renovated Pulman carriage which sits alongside it and does duty now serving quite exceptional cuisine. Good, wholesome food is also offered within the hotel itself, where freshly prepared dishes catering for all appetites are available lunchtime and evening. Guest rooms, as one would expect in a first class establishment, are all en suite and have colour television with video channel, tea and coffee facilities, hairdryer and telephone, and are furnished with sumptuous brass beds. 🏵 🏵 🏵 🏵, *CAMRA.*

GEORGE INN,
Chideock, Bridport,
Dorset DT6 6JD

Tel: 01297 489419

No accommodation; Real ale; Historic interest; Children welcome; Bar and restaurant meals; Car park (50); Lyme Regis 7, Bridport 3.

This traditional Dorset inn nestles amid rolling hills in the picturesque village of Chideock. This is splendid walking country, with many well-kept footpaths giving access to this beautiful part of Dorset. Recently extended in keeping with its old world atmosphere, the George offers everything for the family, including a spacious restaurant with an extensive à la carte menu, two large bars and a family room which leads out onto the sun-trap patio. The menu which is available lunchtime and evenings every day is designed for all tastes, from the favourite local sausage, egg and chips to a very extravagant mixed grill. There are daily specials and filled omelettes are a speciality of the house. Booking is advisable for the Sunday roast dinners. A full range of locally produced beers and lagers is offered, and the carefully chosen wine list includes many favourites from around the world. Customers will be sure of a real Dorset welcome. Credit cards and Switch accepted.

THE MARQUIS OF LORNE,
Nettlecombe, Bridport,
Dorset DT6 3SY

Tel: 01308 485236
Fax: 01308 485666

7 bedrooms, 4 with private bathroom; Palmers House with real ale; Historic interest; Children welcome; Bar food; Car park (50); Bridport 4 miles; ££.

Very popular locally, this friendly, family-run inn offers the full range of what makes a traditional English pub so attractive — well-kept ales, value-for-money food, a cordial welcome and comfortable accommodation. Children are welcome here, and there is a safe play area with trees, swings and climbing frames. Just ten minutes from the Dorset coast, the Marquis of Lorne has seven bedrooms, most en suite, and four different bar/dining areas, each with its own character. The extensive menu and daily-changing specials offer good, wholesome bar snacks as well as more substantial fare, all freshly prepared using local produce wherever possible, including fresh fish. ♛♛ *Commended, AA QQQ Recommended.*

THE THREE ELMS,
North Wootton, Near Sherborne,
Dorset DT9 5JW

Tel: 01935 812881

3 bedrooms; Free House with real ale; Historic interest; Children welcome; Bar and restaurant meals; Car park (100); Sherborne 2 miles; £.

The lush county of Dorset has manifold attractions, not least of which is this lively establishment situated on the A3030 between Sherborne and Sturminster Newton. No fewer than 9 real ales are on offer to tempt the connoisseur, and a good selection of country wines and imported beers ensure that all tastes are catered for. An extensive menu of freshly prepared dishes meets all culinary requirements, and vegetarians will be delighted by the imaginative choice offered, far more than the usual one or two uninspired options one finds so often elsewhere. Three comfortable bedrooms provide bed and breakfast accommodation at extremely competitive rates. *CAMRA Regional Pub of the Year 1993.*

THE THREE HORSESHOES,
Powerstock,
Dorset DT6 3TF
Tel: 01308 485328

4 bedrooms, 2 with private bathroom; J.C. & R.H. Palmer House with real ale; Children welcome; Bar and restaurant meals; Car park (30); Bridport 4 miles; ££.

Rebuilt in local stone after a fire in 1906, the 'Shoes' is set in an attractive garden with fine views over the tranquil Dorset countryside. The bar features cask conditioned ales and scrumpy on draught amongst its wide selection of drinks. The food demands great attention for Pat and Diana Ferguson, your Hosts, have built up a reputation for their marvellous home cooking with fresh local fish, game and lamb favourites with diners. A comprehensive bar snack menu is always available. This is a laid-back sort of place, ideal for winding down. Bees buzz, butterflies flutter by and you can see the cows walking by at milking time. For seekers of such idyllic pleasure, comfortable overnight accommodation is provided and with a full English breakfast, too.

THE BENETT ARMS,
Semley, Shaftesbury,
Dorset SP7 9AS
Tel: 01747 830221
Fax: 01747 830152

5 bedrooms, all with private bathroom; Gibbs Mew House with real ale; Historic interest; Children welcome; Bar and restaurant meals; Car park (40); Shaftesbury 3 miles; ££.

Quietly gazing across the village green, this modest little hostelry is well worth singling out to sample its remarkable range of bar food dishes. Home-cooked steak and kidney pies, local ham, steaks, game and a variety of fish prove exceptional value for money. Selected house wines and a range of cask conditioned ales (no keg beer) will complement meals to perfection. Friendly, informal and devoid of fruit machines, juke boxes, video games and dart boards, this quiet inn, run by Joe Duthie since 1976, is a wonderful holiday retreat for those seeking tranquillity and respite from urban hassle. Good overnight accommodation is available, all rooms having central heating, en suite facilities, colour television, telephone and tea and coffee-makers. *AA, Les Routiers.*

RECOMMENDED SHORT BREAK HOLIDAYS
IN BRITAIN

Introduced by John Carter, TV Holiday Expert and Journalist

Specifically designed to cater for the most rapidly growing sector of the holiday market in the UK. Illustrated details of hotels offering special 'Bargain Breaks' throughout the year.

Available from newsagents and bookshops for £3.60 or direct from the publishers for £4.20 including postage, UK only.

FHG PUBLICATIONS LTD
Abbey Mill Business Centre, Seedhill,
Paisley, Renfrewshire PA1 1TJ

Durham

HIGH FORCE HOTEL,
Forest-in-Teesdale, Barnard Castle,
Durham DL12 0XH

Tel: 01833 622222/622264

8 bedrooms, all with private bathroom; Free House with real ale; Bar food; Car park (20); Middleton-in-Teesdale 5 miles; ££.

Situated opposite England's highest waterfall, this former shooting lodge offers a relaxed atmosphere in which to make a base for whatever your interests may be, whether it is fishing on the River Tees, walking the Pennine Way, tackling Cross Fell, gentle rambles, sightseeing in the local market towns, or simply enjoying the scenery of what is fast becoming one of England's last wildernesses. The bedrooms are fully en suite, and there is a residents' lounge and two comfortable bars, one of which has a blazing log fire during winter months. Bar meals are served lunchtime and evenings, with a daily "specials" board. *ETB* ☙ ☙ ☙.

THREE HORSE SHOES INN,
Running Waters, Sherburn House,
Co. Durham DH1 2SR

Tel: 0191 372 0286

7 bedrooms, all with private bathroom; Free House; Bar and restaurant meals; Car park (50); Durham 4 miles; £££.

Charming hosts Gary and Christine Davis describe the Three Horse Shoes as a comfortable old country inn with a well-stocked cellar, good food and first-class accommodation — and really, that just about sums it up! Guest rooms are attractive indeed, prettily furnished and all en suite, with colour television, tea-making facilities, and central heating. Continental breakfast is available if preferred, but the full English breakfast must be recommended, for it is a truly memorable experience. Evening meals, lunches and bar snacks are served, and the menu includes such delights as individual home-made steak and kidney pies and succulent steaks. *ETB* ☙ ☙ ☙.

PLEASE ENCLOSE A STAMPED
ADDRESSED ENVELOPE WHEN
WRITING TO ENQUIRE ABOUT
ACCOMMODATION FEATURED IN
THIS GUIDE

Essex

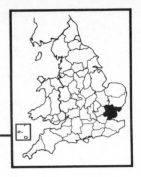

THE QUEENS HEAD INN,
Littlebury, Saffron Walden,
Essex CB11 4TD

Tel: 01799 522251
Fax: 01799 513522

6 bedrooms, all with private bathroom; Free House with real ale; Historic interest; Children welcome; Bar and restaurant meals; Car park (30); Saffron Walden 2 miles; ££.

Mentioned in several leading guides and very popular with real ale aficionados, The Queens Head is all that a traditional English inn should be — but with that certain extra special something that sets it head and shoulders above its fellows. The food is definitely a cut above run-of-the-mill pub grub, with fresh fish taking pride of place on the daily changing menus which can be enjoyed in the dining room or amidst the lively chatter of the bar. The inn plays host to mini beer festivals at regular intervals throughout the year, and patrons can be sure at any time of finding a good selection of real ales on tap, including some local brews. Six freshly decorated en suite bedrooms, including a bridal suite and family room, are available. 🌸 🌸 🌸 *Commended, Logis 2 Chimneys, Good Pub Guide.*

Gloucestershire

THE EIGHT BELLS INN,
Church Street, Chipping Campden,
Gloucestershire GL55 6JG

Tel: 01386 840371

3 bedrooms, all with private bathroom; Free House with real ale; Historic interest; Bar and restaurant meals; Evesham 8 miles; ££.

Built in the 14th century to house the stonemasons and store the bells whilst the church was being built, the Eight Bells has a fascinating history and, even now, is an integral part of the old wool town. It is known that the inn played host to royalty in the past; today, Proprietors, Patrick and Paul Dare will extend a right royal welcome to visitors who come here seeking sustenance and shelter. Mouth-watering lunchtime and evening meals will reward the search, menus being varied and frequently changed and there is a selection of real ales. En suite twin and double bedrooms provide comfortable accommodation and for a Cotswold base full of character, the inn is well worth consideration.

THE OLD NEW INN,
Bourton-on-the-Water,
Gloucestershire GL54 2AF
Tel: 01451 820467

20 bedrooms, 12 with private bathroom; Historic interest; Children welcome; Bar and restaurant meals; Car park (30), garages (6); Gloucester 24 miles, Stow-on-the-Wold 4; ££.

The only trouble with a stay at this gracious establishment is that one is tempted to prolong it indefinitely! Set on the banks of the River Windrush and with charming secluded gardens, the hotel has been run by the Morris family for over fifty years and much has been done to create the friendly, relaxed atmosphere that makes one feel thoroughly at home. Bedrooms are cosy and comfortable, some being available with private facilities, and there is a television room and two lounges exclusively for residents, although many visitors may find themselves drawn to the four public bars where darts or conversation may be enjoyed. A bright and attractive dining room is the setting for a good table d'hôte dinner menu, and light lunches and bar snacks are served at midday. *ETB* ☙ ☙ ☙ *Commended, AA/RAC **, Les Routiers.*

RAGGED COT INN,
Hyde, Chalford, Near Stroud,
Gloucestershire G16 8PE
Tel: 01453 884643/731333
Fax: 01453 731166

10 bedrooms, all with private bathroom; Free House with real ale; Historic interest; Bar and restaurant meals; Car park (55); Stow-on-the-Wold 7 miles; £££.

On one page a printed quotation from the Visitors' Book reads: "He that loveth pleasure shall be a poor man" (Book of Proverbs) and on the next page: "No pleasure ever lasts long enough" (Propertius), which seems to prove that the world is full of frustrated penniless people. A number of them, no doubt, will have been to (and returned to) this charmingly decorated inn deep in the heart of the Cotswolds where there is pleasure in abundance. Guests are subject to most reasonable rates and will have found themselves richer for the experience in mind and body, thus somewhat confounding the theory! Furnished in traditional style with a strong ambience of a mellow past, this lovely inn has warm and friendly bars which are full of character. Bar snacks may be obtained here but for more formal dining, the intimate restaurant offers superb food from an à la carte menu and for which several awards have been won. Vegetarian dishes are also available. Set in unspoilt countryside, this is an ideal touring centre for the Cotswolds and in regal company, too! Gatcombe Park, home of H.R.H. The Princess Royal, is only a mile away and it is only seven miles from Highgrove, H.R.H. Prince Charles' country estate. Beautifully appointed accommodation is a feature of the Ragged Cot, all rooms having en suite facilities, colour television, telephone and hospitality tray and there is a Bridal Suite with a four-poster bed. ☙ ☙ ☙ *Commended.*

WYNDHAM ARMS HOTEL,
Clearwell, Near Coleford,
Gloucestershire GL16 8JT

Tel: 01594 833666
Fax: 01594 836450

17 bedrooms, all with private bathroom; Free House with real ale; Historic interest; Children welcome; Bar and restaurant meals; Car park (50); Frome 8 miles; £££.

In a gentle valley on the edge of the verdant, fairy-tale Royal Forest of Dean, the splendid 600-year-old Wyndham Arms is a recommended centre for a plethora of country pleasures. It is full of old-world charm and although still an inn at heart, now offers inspired hotel facilities, the delicious food served in the busy restaurant and bar being renowned for miles around, home-grown produce figuring prominently. The Rivers Severn and Wye provide fresh salmon in the summer and the chefs are justly proud of their wonderful home-made desserts. Special diets are catered for and children rave about their own 'small persons' menu. Deserving the fullest praise for this happy state of affairs are Proprietors, John and Rosemary Stanford, who fell in love with the place in 1973 and whose West End experience has since served them (and their guests) so well. Elegant guest rooms are delightfully furnished; all have bathrooms en suite, colour television, direct-dial telephone and beverage-making facilities amongst their thoughtful appointments. There are six ground-floor rooms for the less physically able and flat access to the bar and restaurant. For children there are cots and high-chairs and baby-listening intercom. After dining memorably, quiet evenings may be spent, pint or malty dram in hand, chatting with the locals in the cosy bar, perhaps after an excursion to the Wye Valley or Slimbridge Wildfowl Trust, a day's shooting or golf or, hopefully, a winning day at Cheltenham or Chepstow races. *AA/RAC ***, Les Routiers.*

WILD DUCK INN,
Drakes Island, Ewen, Near Cirencester,
Gloucestershire GL7 6BY

Tel: 01285 770310/770364

9 double bedrooms, all with private bathroom; Historic interest; Free House with real ale; Bar and restaurant meals; Car park (50); Chippenham 18 miles, Cheltenham 16, Swindon 16, Tetbury 9, Cirencester 3, Kemble Station 1; £££.

Nestling in delightful, unspoilt Gloucestershire countryside, this is an old inn of outstanding character, with original beams and inglenook open fires giving a traditional atmosphere of warmth and friendliness. Food is of the highest quality, with an extensive menu operating at lunchtime and in the evenings. Bar lunches are also available. Two bedrooms have four-posters and overlook the delightful, award-winning garden. All nine rooms have private bath en suite, colour television, tea/coffee making facilities and telephone, making this a desirable overnight or weekly holiday base, in addition to being an enchanting place to quench one's thirst. Access, Visa, Amex accepted. 🌷 🌷 🌷, *RAC 3 Tankards, Les Routiers Inn of the Year 1994, Logis, Johansens Inn of the Year 1993, Egon Ronay.*

THE HALFWAY HOUSE,
Kineton, Temple Guiting, Near Cheltenham,
Gloucestershire GL54 5UG

Tel: 01451 850344

3 bedrooms; Real ales; Historic interest; Bar and restaurant meals; Car park; Stow-on-the-Wold 6 miles.

This delightful 17th century inn is situated in unspoilt countryside, convenient for visiting Stratford-upon-Avon, Cheltenham, Winchcombe, Burford, Stow-on-the-Wold and Cotswold Farm Park; close to M5. Accommodation is available in two double rooms and one twin room, all with tea/coffee making facilities. There is a small restaurant, and home-made lunches and suppers are served, plus Sunday roast lunches. Special breaks available — details on request from Paul and Katie Hamer.

HUNTERS HALL,
Kingscote, Tetbury,
Gloucestershire GL8 8XZ

Tel: 01453 860393

Fax: 01453 860707

12 bedrooms, all with private bathroom; Free House with real ale; Historic interest; Children welcome; Bar food, restaurant evenings only; Car park; Nailsworth 3 miles; ££££.

Situated midway between Cheltenham and Bath, and central for Bristol, Gloucester and Swindon, Hunters Hall is popular with business persons and tourists alike. Within its creeper-clad walls it provides all that one could require in the way of accommodation and amenities, but in surroundings of unique charm and warmth. An extensive menu of home-made favourites is available each lunchtime and evening in the friendly bar, and the elegant restaurant caters for more formal dining requirements in superb style. Families are welcome here and parents will appreciate the separate play area where a mini assault course is almost guaranteed to tire out the most energetic child while they relax. Inside, decor and furnishings are in keeping with the inn's 16th century origins; rest assured, however, that amenities in the guest bedrooms are right up-to-date, with colour television, direct-dial telephone and tea and coffee making equipment. Two bedrooms are especially suitable for less able guests, and a family suite with cooking facilities is also available. Private functions and business meetings can be accommodated in the Berkeley Room and Gallery, with experienced staff to ensure the smooth running of any event. 🌸 🌸 🌸 🌸, *AA Rosette, Egon Ronay Pub of the Year 1989.*

FOSSEBRIDGE INN,
Fossebridge, Near Cheltenham, Gloucestershire GL54 3JS

Tel: 01285 720721
Fax: 01285 720793

9 bedrooms, all with private bathroom; Free House with real ale; Historic interest; Bar lunches, restaurant evenings only; Car park (25); Cheltenham 12 miles, Northleach 3; ££££.

Diners here are almost spoiled for choice, with no less than three different venues for the enjoyment of the delicious home-cooked fare offered. The River Restaurant and the Bridge Restaurant both present imaginative à la carte menus based on the finest local produce, and a comprehensive bar snack menu with daily changing specials caters for lighter appetites or diners with limited time to spare. With origins as a coaching inn in Tudor times, the Fossebridge is most delightfully situated, with beautiful lawned gardens leading down to the River Coln. If the charm of the Cotswolds prove irresistible, individually styled bedrooms, some with lake and garden views, provide comfortable overnight accommodation.

NEW INN,
Waterley Bottom, North Nibley, Dursley, Gloucestershire GL11 6EF

Tel: 01453 543659

2 bedrooms; Free House with real ale; Bar food; Car park (32); Dursley 2 miles; £.

This sensible and sturdy establishment is especially recommended to real ale enthusiasts, who will find a good selection from a frequently changing list of beers, as well as some unusual bottled beers and rare ciders. Comfortable wheel-backed chairs and high-backed settles in the warm and welcoming lounge with a log fire in winter will encourage visitors to linger over their sampling, and a choice from the good value home-made food menu will complete the experience. Children will be delighted by the play area with swings, slides and a tree-house; parents will be charmed by the beautiful gardens and the peaceful setting.

OREPOOL INN,
St. Briavels Road, Sling, Near Coleford, Gloucestershire GL16 8LH

Tel: 01594 833277
Fax: 01594 833785

10 bedrooms, all with private bathroom; Free House with real ale; Historic interest; Children welcome; Bar food and Sunday lunches; Car park (100); St. Briavels 3 miles; £££.

Bounded by the Rivers Severn and Wye, the Royal Forest of Dean is a mysterious sort of place, stunningly beautiful yet strangely ignored by any but the most imaginative tourists. This is a pity for there is a wealth of interest here and good refreshment and accommodation, too. Dating from the mid-17th century to provide ale for the miners extracting iron ore from the adjacent drift mine, the Orepool Inn is sited on the 'Oreway', a medieval route for the transportation of the ore. The area around the inn is known as the Orepool and tradition has it that the ancient miners traded with the Romans. Today, the discreetly modernised inn dispenses excellent liquid and solid refreshment in a village pub atmosphere, real ale and home-cooked meals being available during all opening hours. Close by, the delightfully furnished chalets of the Orepool Motel are especially well-geared to family parties; all have en suite facilities and have colour television and tea and coffee-makers. Some comprise two interconnecting units, allowing children to sleep within earshot of their parents. Disabled facilities are included in one unit and all walkways and doors throughout the inn are designed for wheelchair access. Other attractions for parents are a baby changing room and plenty of safe open space and a children's play area. One does not need to be a student of industrial archaeology to appreciate the rewards of this lovely area. There are waymarked paths, enchanting woodland glades and streams and interesting flora and fauna. *RAC**, Les Routiers.*

HORSE AND GROOM INN,
Upper Oddington, Moreton-in-Marsh,
Gloucestershire GL56 0XH

Tel: 01451 830584

8 bedrooms, all with private bathroom; Free House with real ale; Historic interest; Children welcome; Bar and restaurant meals; Car park (40); Stow-on-the-Wold 2 miles; ££.

In the very heart of the Cotswolds, this sixteenth-century inn, with its genuine old-world bars and inglenook fireplace, offers the ideal break. Its situation provides the perfect opportunity to explore the villages, historic buildings and places of interest in this delightful area. All bedrooms are en suite, centrally heated and have hot drinks facilities and colour television. Excellent traditional English food is served in the bar and cosy dining room. This is a fine place for families, with a beer garden and a children's garden. Winter break terms available. *HETB* 🏵 🏵 🏵 *Commended.*

THE OLD WHITE LION,
37 North Street, Winchcombe,
Gloucestershire GL54 5PS

Tel: 01242 603300

6 bedrooms, all with private bathroom; Free House with real ale; Historic interest; Bar food, restaurant evenings only; Cheltenham 6 miles; £££.

It was after an unsuccessful day at Cheltenham races that we came across this splendid hostelry — and found we had backed a winner at last. Built in warm Cotswold stone, the Old White Lion dates from the 15th century and performed sterling duty as a coaching inn. Now, tastefully modernised, it still exudes character, emphasised by its stone fireplaces and exposed timbers. You can stay here too, in a well-furnished room with a shower/bath en suite, colour television and tea and coffee-makers. Appetising meals from a comprehensive à la carte menu are served in an attractive restaurant at moderate cost. As a balm from the travails of Cheltenham or as a base for touring the Cotswolds, this gem of an inn certainly has our seal of approval. 🏵 🏵 🏵 *Commended, Egon Ronay.*

Taking a pet on holiday? Then buy
"PETS WELCOME!"

THE ANIMAL LOVERS' HOLIDAY GUIDE
Details of Hotels, Guest Houses, Furnished Accommodation, Caravans, etc. where
holiday makers and their pets are made welcome.
*Available from most newsagents and bookshops price £3.99
or from Publishers (£4.60 including postage, UK only)*
FHG PUBLICATIONS LTD
Abbey Mill Business Centre, Seedhill,
Paisley, Renfrewshire PA1 1TJ

Hampshire

BEACH ARMS HOTEL,
Church Oakley, Near Basingstoke, Hampshire RG23 7EP

Tel: 01256 780210
Fax: 01256 780557

32 bedrooms, all with private bathroom; Allied House; Children welcome; Bar and restaurant meals evenings only; Car park; Basingstoke 5 miles; ££££.

Don't be deceived by the name. This gracious old hotel stands in the gentle countryside of Hampshire, "Beach" being taken from the local family whose forebears include the Father of the House of Commons, W.W. Beach. Thirty-two well appointed en suite bedrooms provide for the overnight guest, and ten rooms have their own special themes, being individually decorated to reflect exotic places or past eras. Even those finding themselves in the Victorian period may be assured of the modern amenities of satellite television, hairdryer, trouser press, telephone, and tea and coffee facilities. Meals may be taken in the bar or restaurant, and an excellent children's menu is offered. 👑 👑 👑 👑

LIONS COURT RESTAURANT AND HOTEL,
29-31 High Street, Fordingbridge, Hampshire SP6 1AS

Tel: 01425 652006
Fax: 01425 657946

6 bedrooms, all with private bathroom; Free House; Historic interest; Children welcome; Car park; Bournemouth 18 miles, Salisbury 11, Ringwood 5; ££/£££.

This charming 17th century family hotel is set on the edge of the New Forest, with all its amenities and rural pursuits. The delightful, sleepy, small town of Fordingbridge is centrally situated for visiting the cathedral city of Salisbury, Bournemouth, Stonehenge, and many other places of interest. There are six en suite bedrooms, one with a four-poster. The à la carte restaurant has a reputation for excellent cuisine in a relaxed, friendly atmosphere. Favouring fresh local produce, specialities include Salad of Smoked Venison and Grilled Calves' Liver with a Bacon and Mushroom Concasse, flavoured with Basil; unusual fish dishes and an extensive vegetarian selection are also available. This is a classic English setting, with gardens extending to the River Avon. Fishing, golf and horse riding are available locally. New Proprietors, Michael and Jennifer Eastick; Chef, Danny Wilson. 👑 👑 👑 *Commended, AA, Les Routiers, Logis.*

YE OLDE GEORGE INN,
Church Street, East Meon, Near Petersfield,
Hampshire

Tel and Fax: 01730 823481

6 bedrooms, all with private bathroom; Free House with real ale; Historic interest; Bar and restaurant meals; Car park; Petersfield 5 miles; ££.

A lovely old hostelry with its restaurant comprising a pair of converted 15th century cottages complete with original inglenook fireplaces and exposed brickwork and beams, the George complements the historic village in which it is situated. The country pub bar invites with its old pine tables, benches, open fires and horse brasses and there is a selection of cask ales and bar food dishes. Night time sees the restaurant at its best with polished tables reflecting the firelight and candleglow as meals chosen from an imaginative à la carte menu and fine wines are given due reverence. Delicious cream teas are served in summer months. The desire may arise to linger longer in this charming place. 👑 👑 👑, *Egon Ronay Recommended.*

HIGH CORNER INN,
Linwood, Near Ringwood,
Hampshire BH24 3QY

Tel: 01425 473973
Fax: 01425 480015

8 bedrooms, all with private bathroom; Free House with real ale; Historic interest; Children and pets welcome; Bar and restaurant meals; Car park; Southampton 18 miles, Bournemouth 17; ££.

A lovely, typically English, early 18th century inn in the very heart of the New Forest, the High Corner Inn gave us a warm feeling of pleasurable anticipation by its very appearance. We were not disappointed; whilst enjoying a leisurely aperitif, we were confronted with a difficult decision in making a lunchtime choice from a wide-ranging bar snacks menu. After a starter, we chose the grilled Avon trout with almonds and a homemade fruit pie to follow. The meal was delicious and we were tempted to return later for an à la carte dinner served in a charming little restaurant. There are rooms for families with children, and a woodland garden, squash court and stables. 🌸🌸 *Commended, Egon Ronay and Les Routiers Recommended.*

WHITE HART HOTEL,
The Square, Whitchurch,
Hampshire RG28 7DN

Tel: 01256 892900
Fax: 01256 896628

18 bedrooms, 10 with private bathroom; Free House with real ale; Historic interest; Bar and restaurant meals; Car park (20); Andover 6 miles; £££.

Steeped in period atmosphere, this traditional coaching inn has been welcoming travellers since 1461. The hospitality and personal service is no less warm and welcoming today. The hotel is widely known for its first-class food whether it be a tasty home-cooked bar snack, a delicious cream tea or an à la carte dish in the charming Lord Denning Restaurant with its genuine Queen Anne ceiling. Judge for yourself! Catering for the modern businessman and casual traveller alike, the White Hart has a variety of period rooms, mostly of Georgian design. The majority have en suite facilities and all have colour television and tea and coffee-makers. Prices, in all respects, are extremely competitive. 🌸🌸, *RAC, Les Routiers.*

THE WYKEHAM ARMS,
75 Kingsgate Street, Winchester,
Hampshire SO23 9PE

Tel: 01962 853834
Fax: 01962 854411

7 bedrooms, all with private bathroom; Eldridge Pope House with real ale; Historic interest; Bar lunches (not Sunday), restaurant evenings only; Car park (12); Southampton 12 miles; ££££.

In the 250 years of its existence, the Wykeham Arms has become more than just a local institution for it attracts visitors from afar. Tucked away in the back streets of this one-time Capital of England, the hostelry is steadfastly traditional in all respects. Four cosy bars, warmed by large log fires, serve real ale (the inn has never served anything else) and magnificent food is produced by a talented team of chefs and for which several awards have been received. Despite its sense of history, the inn is constantly adapting to modern needs but standards of service remain the highest. First-class accommodation is available with en suite bathrooms, colour television, mini-bars, radio/alarm and tea and coffee-making facilities. *Logis, Egon Ronay, RAC.*

THE WOODFALLS INN,
The Ridge, Woodfalls,
Hampshire SP5 2LN

Tel: 01725 513222
Fax: 01725 513220

10 bedrooms, all with private bathroom; Free House with real ale; Children welcome; Bar and restaurant meals; Car park (30); Salisbury 7 miles.

Nestling on the northern edge of the New Forest, on an old route to the cathedral city of Salisbury, this award-winning inn has provided hospitality to travellers since 1870. Ideal for visiting the New Forest, Stonehenge, Romsey and Winchester. After recent refurbishment, all bedrooms are tastefully and individually decorated, with en suite facilities (some with four-poster beds). There is an award-winning restaurant and a bar serving food and real ales. *ETB* 🌺 🌺 🌺 *, AA QQQQQ Premier Selected.*

Herefordshire

THE GREEN MAN,
Fownhope,
Herefordshire HR1 4PE

Tel: 01432 860243
Fax: 01432 860207

15 bedrooms, all with private bathroom; Free House with real ale; Historic interest; Children welcome; Bar food, restaurant evenings only; Car park (80); Gloucester 24 miles, Monmouth 22, Ross-on-Wye 9, Hereford 7; ££.

This ancient black and white timbered inn provides an ideal base for exploring the beautiful surrounding countryside and nearby places of interest. There are two bars, an oak-beamed restaurant, a buttery for bar snacks and a large attractive garden. The resident proprietors place great emphasis upon the quality of food and an informal and friendly atmosphere. An extensive bar food menu is available mornings and evenings, and dinners à la carte are served in the restaurant. Bedrooms all have colour television, radio alarm, direct-dial telephone, tea/coffee making equipment, central heating and many extras. *ETB* 🌺 🌺 🌺 *Commended, AA**, RAC**, Les Routiers, Egon Ronay.*

THE NEW INN,
Market Square, Pembridge, Leominster,
Herefordshire HR6 9DZ

Tel: 01544 388427

6 bedrooms, one with private bathroom; Free House with real ale; Historic interest; Children welcome; Bar food; Car park (30); Kington 6 miles; £.

The last battle of the Wars of the Roses was fought just a few miles from here at Mortimers Cross, and the treaty which gave England's crown to the Yorkist leader is believed to have been signed in the courtroom of this fourteeth century inn. Two ghosts are said to haunt the inn: one a girl, who appears only to women; the other, a red-coated soldier armed with a sword. Comfortable overnight accommodation is available, and a good breakfast is included in the rate for a nicely furnished, spick and span bedroom. A varied and interesting menu is offered at most reasonable prices in the bar, which has a log fire to warm it on chillier days, and the attractive new lounge area is a popular venue for cosy evening dinners. *Egon Ronay.*

YE OLDE SALUTATION INN,
Market Pitch, Weobley,
Herefordshire HR4 8SJ

Tel: 01544 318443

4 bedrooms, all with private bathroom; Free House with real ale; Historic interest; Bar and restaurant meals; Car park; Hereford 12 miles, Leominster 9; £££.

This fine, timber-framed black and white building dates back over 500 years and commands fine views over the medieval village of Weobley, ideally placed for exploring the Welsh Marches, Black Mountains and the Brecon Beacons. Those tempted to linger awhile will find comfortable, centrally heated bedrooms, including a luxury en suite four-poster room. And what could be more pleasant of an evening than a relaxing drink in front of the inglenook fireplace in the lounge bar, while contemplating the delights on offer in the Oak Room Restaurant. Hosts Chris and Frances Anthony take great pride in the freshness and quality of the carefully planned menus presented here, cooking each dish to order and using only the best of local produce. American Express, Visa, Diners and Mastercard accepted. *ETB* ⚘ ⚘ ⚘ *Highly Commended, AA QQQQ.*

THE BUTCHERS ARMS,
Woolhope,
Herefordshire HR1 4RF   Tel: 01432 860281

3 bedrooms; Free House with real ale; Historic interest; Bar food, restaurant Saturday evenings only; Car park (50); Hereford 7 miles; £/££.

Venture along a quiet country lane just past the tiny village of Woolhope and you will find what is surely most people's idea of a real English country inn. Dating from the fourteenth century, the Butchers Arms offers a warm welcome to locals and visitors alike, plus good food and refreshment to those in search of such. The intimate restaurant is open on Saturday evenings, offering an interesting selection of traditional and more unusual dishes, all featuring the best of local produce. Bar meals and snacks are available at lunchtimes and in the evenings, along with a good range of traditional ales, ciders etc. Spotlessly clean, comfortable accommodation can be obtained at most reasonable rates. *AA, Egon Ronay.*

Hertfordshire

JESTER HOTEL,
Odsey, Near Ashwell,
Hertfordshire SG7 5RS   Tel and Fax: 01462 742011

14 bedrooms, all with private bathroom; Free House with real ale; Children welcome; Bar and restaurant meals; Car park (40); Royston 4 miles; £££.

Although possessing all the attributes of a country hotel, The Jester remains, at heart, the rural pub from which it grew. Certainly, it retains its original ambience even though it now boasts superb guest rooms with private bathrooms, colour television and direct-dial telephones amongst their appointments. One special room has a four-poster bed — honeymooners please note. With French windows leading to a delightful garden, the convivial lounge bar is an ideal setting for a drink or snack with a roaring log fire to add cheer in winter. Acquaintance with the restaurant is definitely recommended for its interesting à la carte menu. Flambés are a speciality of the house, with the traditional Sunday lunch an affordable treat for all the family. *Les Routiers, Club Bon Viveur.*

WHITE HART,
High Street, Puckeridge,
Hertfordshire SG11 1RR

Tel: 01920 821309

No accommodation; McMullens House with real ale; Historic interest; Children welcome; Bar and restaurant meals; Car park (50); Ware 6 miles, Bishops Stortford 6.

This pleasant and unpretentious pub offers a challenge to the gluttonous — finish the chef's seafood platter and win a voucher that can be used towards the next meal! With some regret we declined, opting instead for a prime rump steak with wine and mushroom sauce, and spinach and mushroom lasagne, one of the many vegetarian choices available. Both were beautifully prepared and presented, and their value for money could not be denied. Hot and cold snacks are served daily in the bar, while those opting for the extensive à la carte menu may choose to eat in the lounge or dining room, where children are welcomed and well catered for. *Relais Routiers, Runner Up 1990 Guinness Best Pub Food Awards.*

Humberside

BRIGGATE LODGE INN,
Ermine Street, Broughton, Brigg,
South Humberside DN20 0NQ

Tel: 01652 650770
Fax: 01652 650495

50 bedrooms, all with private bathroom; Free House with real ale; Children welcome; Bar and restaurant meals; Car park; Brigg 3 miles; ££££.

Literally just yards from Junction 4 on the M180, this spacious modern building houses every amenity the weary traveller could wish for. Food is served from 7am until very late in the light and airy Buttery, and for those with more time on their hands, à la carte and table d'hôte menus are presented in the elegant restaurant which affords lovely views of the surrounding woodland. Bedrooms are tastefully decorated and equipped with all the facilities expected by today's discerning visitor, and there are two ground floor rooms with adjacent parking which are especially designed for the disabled. Those in search of refreshment can enjoy morning coffee or afternoon tea, or perhaps a relaxing drink in the comfortable and friendly bars. ♥ ♥ ♥ ♥ ♥ *Highly Commended, AA and RAC***.*

THE FEATHERS,
Market Place, Pocklington,
Humberside YO4 2AH

Tel: 01759 303155
Fax: 01759 304382

12 bedrooms, all with private bathroom; Scottish & Newcastle House with real ale; Historic interest; Bar and restaurant meals; Car park (60); York 9 miles; ££/£££.

Once a coaching inn, this comfortable and tastefully modernised establishment stands on the site where an inn has existed since Elizabethan times. With its timbers, wrought iron and natural stonework, the lounge bar exudes a warm welcome aided by the warmth of an open fire in cooler weather. The Feathers is conveniently placed in the centre of this small and pleasant town, within easy reach of York and the coastal resorts of Scarborough and Bridlington. Comfortable accommodation is available in the main building and in the annexe, all rooms having private facilities and television. Table d'hôte and à la carte luncheons and dinners are served daily in the pleasant dining room.

Isle of Wight

CLARENDON HOTEL AND WIGHT MOUSE INN,
Chale,
Isle of Wight PO38 2HA
Tel: 01983 730431

14 bedrooms, two family suites, 8 with private bathroom or shower; Free House with real ales; Historic interest; Children most welcome; Bar and restaurant meals; Car park (200); Newport 9 miles, Ventnor 7; ££.

Our Hotel, The Clarendon, is a 17th century Coaching Inn of immense charm and character enjoying an enviable reputation for excellent food, wine, comfort and hospitality. Standing in its own lovely grounds, it overlooks the magnificent West Wight coastline and is surrounded by beautiful National Trust countryside. Children are very welcome, at reduced rates, and we are a few minutes from Blackgang Chine and several beautiful beaches. We have absolutely everything for your comfort. All rooms have colour television and tea and coffee making facilities, and all bathrooms have hairdryers. **Our Pub, The Wight Mouse Inn,** which is attached to the hotel, was awarded the Egon Ronay Family Pub of the Year Award in 1990. It has great atmosphere, open fires, six real ales, 365 different whiskies, excellent meals and live entertainment nightly all year round, and is open all day every day for meals and drinks. Golf, Shooting, Fishing, and Car Hire can all be easily arranged and our Hotel has its own riding stables. For a brochure and full details please write to John and Jean Bradshaw. *ETB* 🌷 🌷 🌷 *Commended, Egon Ronay, AA**, RAC**, Les Routiers, Good Pub Guide "UK Whisky Pub of the Year" 1994, CAMRA and Ashley Courtenay Recommended.*

SPYGLASS INN,
The Esplanade, Ventnor,
Isle of Wight PO38 1JX

Tel: 01983 855338

3 suites; Free House with real ale; Historic interest; Children welcome; Bar and restaurant meals; Car park; Shanklin 3 miles; £££/££££.

Yo, ho, ho and a bottle of what you fancy — to go with your choice of freshly prepared fare from the extensive menu and served in a nautical environment. This fine seafront hostelry is renowned for its magnificent cuisine with seafood, naturally, a speciality of the house. One of the most famous inns on the delectable island, the Spyglass is a happy, friendly place to visit with entertainments and special events held regularly. Conviviality reigns in the bar, a mood to which a glass or two of the fine real ales contributes not a little. Bed and Breakfast accommodation is provided in three self-contained suites comprising a double bedroom with bathroom en suite and a lounge and patio with wide sea views. *Egon Ronay Recommended.*

Kent

THE STAR AND EAGLE HOTEL,
High Street, Goudhurst,
Kent TN17 1AL

Tel: 01580 211512

11 bedrooms, 9 with private bathroom; Whitbread House with real ale; Historic interest; Children welcome; Bar and restaurant meals; Car park (25); Cranbrook 4 miles; £££.

Enjoying stunning views over the Kentish Weald, the 14th century Star and Eagle was once linked by a tunnel to the medieval church of this most attractive village and was used as a base by smugglers. Pleasantly furnished and comfortable accommodation is available, including a full English breakfast, en suite guest rooms having television, radio, beverage-making facilities and early morning call system. Excellent luncheons and dinners are served to residents and non-residents alike in the popular restaurant in addition to a variety of lunchtime bar snacks.

THE RINGLESTONE INN,
Harrietsham, Near Maidstone, Kent ME17 1NX

Tel: 01622 859900
Fax: 01622 859966

No accommodation; Free House with real ale; Historic interest; Children welcome; Bar lunches, restaurant; Car park (50); Leeds Castle 3 miles.

Since the early 1600s this unique inn has offered a "ryghte joyouse and welcome greetynge to ye all", and still today its original brick and flint walls, sturdy oak beams, inglenooks and traditional wooden furniture reflect the relaxed atmosphere of less hurried times. Highly recommended in most good food guides since 1984, the Ringlestone offers superb "help yourself" buffet lunch and interesting evening menus, featuring the best of local produce. Those in search of refreshment will savour the selection of well-kept real ales and the interesting range of English country fruit wines and champagnes — something really different! Set in two acres of peaceful gardens deep in the lush Kent countryside, this truly welcoming inn upholds the finest traditions of English inn-keeping. Amex, Diner, Visa and Mastercard accepted.

LIME TREE HOTEL AND RESTAURANT,
The Limes, The Square, Lenham, Kent ME17 2PQ

Tel: 01622 859509
Fax: 01622 850096

7 bedrooms, all with private bathroom; Historic interest; Children welcome; Bar and restaurant meals; Car park; Charing 4 miles; £££.

Recently refurbished throughout, the hotel still retains its traditional features, the original timber-framed building dating back to the 14th century. Within easy reach of the M20 and the Channel Tunnel, the Lime Tree Hotel and its famous restaurant lies in a picturesque village in the heart of the Garden of England. Historic Canterbury is only a short drive away and beautiful Leeds Castle is within five miles. The delightful restaurant, one of the best in the area, presents an extensive à la carte menu specialising in classic French and Continental cuisine. First-class accommodation is available in comfortable en suite bedrooms, all with colour television, direct-dial telephone and beverage-making facilities. *Les Routiers.*

The **£** symbol when appearing at the end of the italic section of an entry shows the anticipated price, during 1995, for **single full Bed and Breakfast.**

Under £30	£	**Over £45 but under £60**	£££
Over £30 but under £45	££	**Over £60**	££££

This is meant as an indication only and does not show prices for Special Breaks, Weekends, etc. Guests are therefore advised to verify all prices on enquiring or booking.

THE GREEN MAN,
Shatterling, Wingham, Canterbury,
Kent CT3 1JR
Tel: 01304 812525

4 bedrooms, one with private bathroom; Free House with real ale; Bar and restaurant meals; Car park; Canterbury 7 miles; £/£££.

The archetypal English country inn with all the traditional values, "The Green Man" has several qualities that place it above many of its fellows. On the A257 and set amongst the hop fields and orchards of South-East Kent, it is conveniently near Canterbury, the ports of Dover and Folkestone, and the Channel Tunnel. Granted an ale licence in 1820, it has grown impressively into a fully residential hostelry and restaurant with a deserved reputation for its comfortable accommodation, wide selection of real ales, hot and cold bar snacks and straightforward and reasonably priced à la carte menu. Friendly and informal, and a wayside inn in the truest sense, "The Green Man" is a fine example. *Les Routiers, Good Beer Guide.*

SHIP INN & SMUGGLERS RESTAURANT,
Conyer Quay, Teynham, Near Sittingbourne,
Kent ME9 9HR
Tel: 01795 521404
Fax: 01795 521820

No accommodation; Free House with real ale; Historic interest; Bar and restaurant meals; Faversham 4 miles.

Claiming to stock the greatest range of drinks of any pub or restaurant in Britain, The Ship is a fascinating old inn, with an absorbing history. On the edge of a winding backwater off the Swale, Conyer had an infamous reputation for smuggling in the 17th and 18th centuries and, as one local journalist wrote: ". . . if the Barge Bar of The Ship Inn at Conyer could talk, it would have some merry tales to tell!". The building, built in 1642, was, in the main part, a baker's shop, indeed, the original oven may be seen alongside the inglenook fireplace. Next door was the blacksmith's, that is now the famed Smugglers Restaurant. The blacksmith successfully applied for an ale house licence in 1802, whilst his neighbour continued baking bread until 1832. At this time, the owner of The Ship Inn, as it had been named, bought the baker's shop and the whole building was upgraded to a tavern. Since then, generations of regulars, and thousands of visitors — by road and by sea — have gravitated here to marvel at, and enjoy, the almost bewildering selection of solid and liquid refreshment. A stock of 250 whiskies (including 175 malts) has spawned the unique *Malt Whisky Trail;* the number of traditional ales served in The Ship Inn is legendary, and regular beer festivals are held. More than 300 wines, from around the world, have achieved several awards and, with more than 100 served 'By the Glass', the fabulous Smugglers Restaurant is the ideal place to experiment. Would-be gourmets haven't lived until they have ventured down to Conyer Quay. *Les Routiers.*

CHASER INN AND RESTAURANT,
Stumble Hill, Shipbourne, Tonbridge,
Kent TN11 9PE

Tel: 01732 810360
Fax: 01732 810941

15 bedrooms, all with private bathroom; Free House with real ale; Historic interest; Children welcome; Bar and restaurant meals; Car park (30); Tonbridge 4 miles; ££££.

This unusual inn sets its porticoed facade to gaze amicably across the village green. Close examination proves it to be, in essence, the perfect country inn, the name of which bears reference to the late Peter Cazalet, trainer of the Queen Mother's steeplechasers, whose stables were close by. An extensive and imaginative range of dishes is on offer in an impressive restaurant with a beamed, vaulted ceiling and panelled walls. Situated in the Garden of England with easy access to London, the coast and a verdant countryside rich in history, this is an excellent place for a holiday of some variety. Bedrooms are all en suite and have a television and direct-dial telephone. 🐦🐦🐦 *Commended, AA QQQQ Selected, Les Routiers.*

THE BULL HOTEL,
Wrotham, Near Sevenoaks,
Kent TN15 7RF

Tel: 01732 885522
Fax: 01732 886288

10 bedrooms, 6 with private bathroom; Free House with real ale; Historic interest; Bar and restaurant meals; Car park (50); London 27 miles, Maidstone 11, Sevenoaks 7; £££.

The Bull Hotel is a family-run fourteenth century coaching inn of great charm and character in the historic village of Wrotham. It was once a stopping-off point for pilgrims on their way to Canterbury. It specialises in comfortable accommodation and superb cooking at reasonable prices, with an à la carte restaurant, set menus and home-made bar snacks. All rooms have colour television, telephone and tea-making facilities. Ideal as a base for visiting London and places of local interest — just off M20 and M25/26, 40 minutes by train to London, near Channel ports and Gatwick. *ETB* 🐦🐦🐦 *Commended, AA Listed.*

Lancashire

THE BLUE ANCHOR,
68 Main Street, Bolton-le-Sands, Carnforth,
Lancashire LA5 8DN

Tel: 01524 823241
Fax: 01524 824745

4 bedrooms, all with private bathroom; Mitchells House with real ale; Children welcome; Bar food, restaurant evenings only; Car park (4); Lancaster 5 miles; ££.

This sturdy stone-built inn makes an ideal base for those wishing to explore both the Lake District and the seaside attractions of Morecambe and the North West coast, situated as it is in the picturesque village of Bolton-le-Sands, with easy access from the M6 motorway. The cosy, freshly decorated bedrooms all have private facilities, colour television, tea/coffee makers and hairdryers, making a stay here, however long or short, a real pleasure. Those seeking refreshment will find their needs amply met by the extensive bar menu available each lunchtime and evening, with a good value table d'hôte menu providing additional choice. 🏵 🏵 🏵 *Commended.*

THE STRAWBURY DUCK HOTEL,
Overshores Road, Entwistle, Near Bolton,
Lancashire BL7 0LU

Tel: 01204 852013

4 bedrooms, all with private bathroom; Free House with real ale; Historic interest; Children welcome; Bar food (closed Monday lunchtime except Bank Holidays); Car park; Manchester 10 miles; ££.

Small and cosy and bursting with old-fashioned charm, this welcoming free house sits comfortably by the Manchester/Blackburn railway line and offers four nicely furnished guest bedrooms to the weary traveller, three with four-poster bed and all with full en suite facilities and tea/coffee making. Bar fare ranges from sandwiches to genuine Aberdeen Angus steaks served on a hot sizzle plate. Also a choice of vegetarian dishes and a wide range of authentic Indian cuisine. Pub renowned for fine selection of hand-drawn real ales (weekly guest beers).

BAYLEY ARMS HOTEL,
Hurst Green, Near Whalley,
Lancashire BB7 9QB

Tel: 01254 826478

Fax: 01254 826797

8 bedrooms, all with private bathroom; Free House with real ale; Bar and restaurant meals; Car park; Preston 13 miles, Clitheroe 5; £££.

In the heart of the picturesque Ribble Valley and adjacent to Stonyhurst College, the Bayley Arms has recently undergone complete refurbishment in the hands of Owners, Michael and Krystyna Taylor, although every care has been taken to retain all the original features and the welcoming log fires and beamed ceilings remain. In the handsome bars, meals and snacks are available as well as real cask ales, wines and spirits at reasonable prices. Tempting chef-prepared à la carte dishes, including daily specials, are available every day. Attractive en suite bedrooms, including two family rooms, provide splendid overnight accommodation, all rooms with colour television and tea-making facilities. 🍃🍃🍃 *Commended, Les Routiers.*

Leicestershire

MARQUESS OF EXETER HOTEL,
Main Street, Lyddington, Near Uppingham,
Leicestershire LE15 9LT

Tel: 01572 822477

Fax: 01572 821342

17 bedrooms, all with private bathroom; Free House with real ale; Historic interest; Children welcome; Bar and restaurant meals; Car park (80); Leicester 27 miles, Kettering 13; ££££.

Close to Rutland Water, this fine sixteenth-century coaching inn is a careful blend of old world character, quality cuisine and smart, beautifully appointed accommodation which caters well for tourist and businessman alike. The usual range of bar meals and snacks is served between 12.15 and 1.45pm and again from 7.15 until 10pm in the snug beamed bar, and the traditionally furnished restaurant is open Monday to Friday lunchtime and Monday to Saturday evening, offering a choice of à la carte and table d'hôte menus, as well as for Sunday luncheon. En suite bathroom, trouser press, hairdryer, direct-dial telephone, beverage facilities and colour television are standard in all the tastefully decorated bedrooms. There are two suites with private lounge. Weekend breaks available. 🍃🍃🍃🍃, *AA and RAC ***, Les Routiers.*

Lincolnshire

MASONS ARMS,
Cornmarket, Louth,
Lincolnshire LN11 9PY

Tel: 01507 609525/6

10 bedrooms, 5 with private bathroom; Free House with real ale; Historic interest; Children welcome; Bar lunches, restaurant Wed.-Sat. evenings, plus Sat. and Sun. lunch; Grimsby 14 miles; ££.

A family-run old coaching inn offering friendly service and amenities at affordable prices, the Masons Arms is ideally situated between the Lincolnshire Wolds and coast, an area of unspoiled and largely undiscovered beauty. For a holiday that is just that bit different or even a fleeting visit, this interesting old posting house is well recommended. Recently sympathetically refurbished by Proprietors, Mike and Margaret Harrison, the hostelry has admirably equipped guest rooms although restoration has not diminished its character and ambience. The period-style bars retain their warm appeal and delicious home-made meals are available in the elegant Pentalpha Restaurant, including vegetarian dishes. ♛ ♛ ♛ *Commended, AA QQQQ, Egon Ronay, CAMRA.*

WHITE HART INN,
Tetford, Near Horncastle,
Lincolnshire LN9 6QQ

Tel: 01507 533255

7 bedrooms; Free House with real ale; Historic interest; Children welcome; Bar food; Car park; Skegness 17 miles, Horncastle 6.

In olden times this little Wolds village on the River Lymm had four inns; now only the sixteenth century White Hart remains, proof perhaps of the survival of the fittest! One interesting feature which must be seen and admired is the large oak settle by the fireplace, one of the few to have survived to the present day and thought to have been used by Dr Johnson on his 1764 visit to address the Tetford Club, in addition to having supported the illustrious posterior of Alfred, Lord Tennyson. Real home-cooked meals are available every evening, and good bar snacks are served both lunchtime and evening — delicious with a pint of real ale.

Middlesex

THE SWAN,
Village Road, Denham, Near Uxbridge, Middlesex UB9 5BH

Tel: 01895 832085

No accommodation; Courage House with real ale; Historic interest; Bar lunches; Car park; Uxbridge 2 miles.

Out for a family run or touring in the area? Then leave the M40 at Junction 1 and follow the signs to this pretty little village, where this friendly hostelry provides good food and a warm welcome. Refreshments on offer include well kept real ales on handpump, the perfect accompaniment to the tasty sandwiches and good value hot dishes available each lunchtime. There is a large garden (floodlit in the evenings), with picnic tables and a children's play house, while donkeys survey the scene from the adjacent paddock.

Norfolk

THE OLD RAM COACHING INN,
Ipswich Road (A140), Tivetshall St Mary, Norfolk NR15 2DE

Tel: 01379 676794
Fax: 01379 608399

5 bedrooms, all with en suite bathroom; Free House with real ale; Historic interest; Children welcome; Bar and restaurant meals; Car park (120); Harleston 6 miles; ££££.

This attractive 17th century coaching inn has several elevated eating areas, including a designated non-smoking dining room. The spacious main room has red brick floors, stripped beams and a huge log fire in the brick hearth. An intimate dining room known as the Coach House boasts cosy pew seating, leading to a gallery featuring Victorian copper and brassware. The emphasis is very much on food (breakfast, lunch and dinner are served), with some tables reserved on weekdays and weekends. All the luxury en suite bedrooms have satellite television, telephone, hairdryer, trouser press and tea/coffee making facilities and are furnished to an excellent standard. No dogs. *ETB* 👑 👑 👑 *Highly Commended, RAC Merit Award, AA QQQQ Selected, Egon Ronay Recommended.*

SARACEN'S HEAD INN AND EATING HOUSE,
Wolterton, Near Erpingham,
Norfolk NR11 7LX   Tel: 01263 768909

3 bedrooms, all with private bathroom; Free House with real ale; Historic interest; Bar and restaurant meals; Car park; Erpingham 1 mile; ££.

A free house with a delightful courtyard and walled garden, the Saracen's Head is well recommended for its delicious and reasonably-priced food, made even more enjoyable by the casual atmosphere in which it may be appreciated — no piped music, no fruit machines! During the year a series of Feasts is organised in the long tabled Upper Room. The ideal place for a quiet fun night out, the inn and its increasingly popular Eating House is within half-an-hour's drive from Norwich. It is a trifle difficult to find but well worth the effort. Erpingham lies a mile or so to the west of the A140 Aylsham — Cromer road and is signposted. From there a further sign points to Wolterton (not marked on most maps).

Northamptonshire

THE RED LION HOTEL,
East Haddon,   Tel: 01604 770223
Northamptonshire NN6 8BU   Fax: 01604 645866

5 bedrooms; Charles Wells House with real ale; Historic interest; Children welcome; Bar and restaurant meals; Car park; Northampton 8 miles.

This traditional, stone-built inn sits snugly in the charming village of East Haddon, just seven miles from Junction 18 on the M1 and 8 miles from Northampton. Leisure facilities in the area are excellent — golf, fishing, squash, swimming and snooker are all available locally. Those wishing to make the most of a relaxing weekend break will find comfortable, spick-and-span bedrooms. Good English cooking is the basis of the carefully balanced à la carte menu and a comprehensive range of snacks is available at lunchtime and in the evening. Lighter appetites are well catered for in the brass and copper bedecked bars, with a tasty range of home-made bar snacks, accompanied by one's choice from the well-kept ales, beers, wines and other refreshments. *Egon Ronay, Good Food Guide.*

THE GLOBE HOTEL,
High Street, Weedon, Northampton, Northamptonshire NN7 4QD

Tel: 01327 340336
Fax: 01327 349058

18 bedrooms, all with private bathroom; Free House; Historic interest; Bar and restaurant meals; Car park (40); Daventry 4 miles; £.

Weedon Village, at the very heart of England, was for many years a cavalry training centre, particularly during the Napoleonic Wars. The Globe itself dates from that time and has been totally refurbished by Peter and Penny Walton to a most comfortable standard, whilst still retaining its historic character. All 18 rooms are fully equipped and are en suite. We offer a Weekend Giveaway Break Bed and Breakfast rate of only £19.95 per person per night. Situated on the crossroads of the A5/A45, three miles west of Junction 16 of the M1, within easy touring distance of Warwick Castle, Leamington Spa, Stratford-upon-Avon, Naseby Battlefield, Althorp House (Princess Diana's ancestral home), Stoke Bruerne Waterways Centre and Museum, and Silverstone Grand Prix Circuit. Our comprehensive food operation OPEN ALL DAY features a home fayre bar meals menu, pies (our speciality) and a value-for-money à la carte menu. Send for our free tour and information pack. 🌑🌑🌑🌑 *Commended.*

Northumberland

CAT INN,
Great North Road (A1), Cheswick, Berwick-upon-Tweed, Northumberland TD15 2RL

Tel: 01289 387251

8 bedrooms, 5 with private bathroom; Free House with real ale; Historic interest; Children welcome; Bar and restaurant meals; Car park (40); Berwick-upon-Tweed 5 miles; £.

A welcome sight on the Great North Road, south of Berwick-upon-Tweed, the Cat was once part of an 18th century farmhouse of the same name. Surrounded by open fields and only 1½ miles from the sea, the hospitable hostelry is just the place to stop for delicious meals and good ale. It is justly popular with anglers and golfers, excellent opportunities for which exist nearby. Also situated for exploring the Border Country, the inn provides first-rate and reasonably-priced overnight accommodation, most of the rooms having en suite facilities with a full English breakfast to look forward to in the morning. 🌑🌑🌑, *Les Routiers.*

BLACK BULL INN,
Main Street, Lowick, Berwick-upon-Tweed,
Northumberland TD15 2UA
Tel: 01289 88228

3 bedrooms, all with private bathroom; Free House with real ale; No children under 14 for accommodation; Bar lunches, restaurant meals; Car park (40); Wooler 7 miles; ££.

Just off the A1, south of Berwick-upon-Tweed, the Black Bull is ideally placed for a variety of interesting tourist attractions. So when visiting Holy Island (5 miles), imposing Bamburgh Castle (11 miles), the lovely Tweed Valley or the Cheviots, take time out to call at this comfortable and friendly country inn to sample its excellent ale and reasonably-priced home-cooked food. However, such is the popularity of the fare, it is advisable to book in advance. Originally a 17th century inn, the Black Bull was extended in Victorian times and further improved by present incumbents, Anne and Tom Grundy, who have recently added a fine, 66-seater dining room and three en suite bedrooms. There is a well-furnished, self-contained cottage adjacent to the pub. *ETB Recommended, Les Routiers, Egon Ronay Recommended.*

OLDE SHIP HOTEL,
Seahouses,
Northumberland
Tel: 01665 720200

15 bedrooms, all with private bathroom; Free House with real ale; Children welcome; Bar lunches, restaurant meals; Car park (12); Berwick-upon-Tweed 22 miles, Alnwick 14; £££.

Old-fashioned in a sense, this homely old inn was originally built as a farmhouse in the mid-eighteenth century. The Olde Ship stands above the picturesque harbour and has a long established reputation for excellent food and drink. Because of the nautical theme throughout one may be tempted to linger longer in this fascinating hostelry. All guest rooms, including two with four-poster beds, are en suite and have telephone and satellite colour television. Mr and Mrs A.C. Glen personally supervise the well-being of their guests, and for a holiday break in convivial surroundings this little place has much to commend it. Courtesy coach from local station. The local Rotary Club meets at the Olde Ship on Tuesday evenings.

TANKERVILLE ARMS HOTEL,
Cottage Road, Wooler,
Northumberland NE71 6AD
Tel: 01668 281581
Fax: 01668 281387

17 bedrooms, all with private bathroom; Historic interest; Bar and restaurant meals; Car park; Alnwick 15 miles; ££.

A charming 17th century Coaching Inn with a warm and friendly atmosphere situated in the heart of the Northumbrian countryside. An ideal base for the unspoilt attractions of Bamburgh, Holy Island, the Cheviots and the Scottish Borders. Fine food, excellent service, quality bedrooms and a strong desire to make your stay both enjoyable and memorable. The Tankerville Arms Hotel is situated just off the A697 in Wooler, Northumberland. 🐾🐾🐾🐾 *Highly Commended, AA and RAC**.*

Nottinghamshire

WILLOW TREE INN,
Front Street, Barnby-in-the-Willows, Newark,
Nottinghamshire NG24 2SA

Tel. and Fax: 01636 626613

5 bedrooms, 2 with private bathroom; Free House with real ale; Historic interest; Children welcome; Bar and restaurant meals; Car park (50); Newark 4 miles; £/££.

A charming little village inn built at the turn of the 18th century, the homely Willow Tree is well known for its quality food and the traditional ales served in its heavily-beamed bar. Situated in a conservation area and within a short drive of Nottingham, Lincoln and Sherwood Forest as well as nearby 12th-15th century Newark Castle, this is a gem of a place in which to stay, comfortable accommodation being available at most moderate rates. Sporting attractions locally include golf, horse riding and excellent fishing on the Trent and Witham. The 24 cover à la carte restaurant offers a wide choice of tempting dishes including several home-made country specialities. *RAC Listed, AA QQ, CAMRA.*

Please mention
Recommended WAYSIDE INNS
when seeking refreshment or
accommodation at a Hotel
mentioned in these pages

Oxfordshire

THE KING'S HEAD INN AND RESTAURANT,
Bledington, Near Kingham,
Oxfordshire OX7 6HD   Tel and Fax: 01608 658365

12 bedrooms, all with private bathroom; Free House with real ale; Historic interest; Children welcome; Bar food, restaurant evenings only; Car park (70); Stow-on-the-Wold 4 miles; ££.

Facing Bledington's village green with its brook and ducks (all known locally by name!) stands the King's Head Inn, an establishment which has echoed with the sounds of convivial hospitality for over four centuries. Bledington nestles in the heart of the Cotswolds and is in easy reach of Stratford, Bourton-on-the-Water and Burford. The charming accommodation is in keeping with the atmosphere, all bedrooms having en suite bathroom, television, telephone and hot drinks facilities. High quality and inventive bar fare is served, with full à la carte in the restaurant in the evenings. Real ale is served in the two bars with their inglenook fireplaces and original beams, while a garden room and garden add to this delightful old inn. *ETB 3 Crowns Commended, Johansens, Egon Ronay, AA, Logis.*

THE ROEBUCK INN,
Drayton, Banbury,
Oxfordshire OX15 6EN   Tel: 01295 730542

2 bedrooms; Free House with real ale; Historic interest; Bar food, restaurant evenings only; Car park; Banbury 2 miles; ££.

Four hundred years of history have contributed to the unique character of this welcoming little inn which serves the needs of the local community and of patrons from farther afield, drawn here by virtue of the excellent food and well-kept traditional ales. Dining here is a particular pleasure, whether it is a light snack amidst the lively chatter of the bar, or a more leisurely evening dinner in the cosy restaurant. Whatever your choice, rest assured that it has been freshly prepared from the choicest ingredients, with that extra touch of flair in the presentation that sets the Roebuck head and shoulders above its competitors. Traditional ales are included in the range of refreshments available, and two neat bedrooms provide cosy overnight accommodation. *Egon Ronay, Good Beer Guide, Les Routiers.*

SHEPHERDS HALL INN,
Witney Road, Freeland,
Oxfordshire OX8 8HQ
Tel: 01993 881256

5 bedrooms, all with private bath or shower and toilet; Free House with real ale; Children welcome; Bar food; Car park (50); Oxford 12 miles, Witney 4, Woodstock 4; ££.

One of the finest houses for miles, the welcoming Shepherds Hall stands on the A4095 Woodstock to Witney road, in an area famed for its sheep rearing, hence its name. Rooms are now modernised, with colour TV, direct-dial telephones and tea/coffee making facilities, yet retain the atmosphere of a true country inn, and proprietors Liz and David Fyson present a comprehensive selection of appetising meals and snacks in the bar every day. This is a good place to bring the family (perhaps after visiting Woodstock and Blenheim Palace) for there is an attractive beer garden and children's play area. Wholesome accommodation is available at reasonable rates and this includes a full English breakfast. *HETB* 👑 👑.

THE DOG HOUSE HOTEL,
Frilford Heath, Near Marcham, Abingdon,
Tel: 01865 390830
Oxfordshire OX13 6QJ
Fax: 01865 390860

19 bedrooms, all with private bathroom; Morland House with real ale; Children welcome; Bar and restaurant meals; Car park; Abingdon 4 miles; ££££.

It is seldom that one would claim to be delighted to be "in the dog house" but when the establishment in question is this sturdy stone-built inn, a stay here is a privilege, not a punishment! The attractively furnished bedrooms, all en suite, offer a full range of facilities, and special Friday and Saturday rates make a weekend break a particularly attractive proposition. The Hotel Restaurant offers an extensive choice of menu with the emphasis very firmly on quality and professional service; meals can be enjoyed in the light and airy conservatory or in the bar, where a range of blackboard specials prove excellent value for money. The golfing enthusiast will be delighted to find two 18-hole courses almost next door.

FALKLAND ARMS,
Great Tew,
Tel: 01608 683653
Oxfordshire OX7 4DB
Fax: 01608 683656

4 bedrooms, 3 with private bathroom; Free House with real ale; Historic interest; Bar lunches; Car park (30); Chipping Norton 5 miles.

Set in a lovely village about five miles from Chipping Norton, this Grade I Listed building is most appealing, and quite deservedly is mentioned in several leading pub and food guides. It is impossible to say what is most attractive — the wonderful, old-fashioned style of the place, the superb range of traditional English ales which includes regularly changing guest beers, the country wines and farm ciders, or the lunchtime bar food, all home-made, with traditional favourites supplemented by daily specials. Limited accommodation is available for those who simply cannot tear themselves away — but such is this enchanting inn's popularity, rooms must be booked well in advance.

WHITE HART HOTEL,
Nettlebed, Near Henley-on-Thames,
Tel: 01491 641245
Oxfordshire RG9 5DD
Fax: 01491 641423

6 bedrooms, all with private bathroom; Brakspear House with real ale; Historic interest; Children welcome; Bar and restaurant meals; Car park (40); Henley-on-Thames 5 miles; ££££.

This sixteenth century coaching inn on the A4130 Henley to Oxford road is a real wayside hostelry with all the traditional values. That said, its accommodation now adheres to the highest modern standards, all rooms having en suite facilities, colour television, direct-dial telephone and hospitality tray. Indeed, it is indicative of the warmth of welcome that each guest will find a glass of sherry and a fruit bowl awaiting them to celebrate their arrival. And there is plenty to celebrate here for, apart from the conviviality of the bars with their roaring log fires, good company and first-class refreshment, there is a top-class restaurant offering a mouth-watering selection of dishes. *ETB* 👑 👑 👑 👑, *RAC Highly Acclaimed.*

THE BIRD IN HAND,
Hailey, Witney,
Oxfordshire OX8 5XP

Tel: 01993 868321
Fax: 01993 868702

16 bedrooms, all with private bathroom; Free House with real ale; Historic interest; Bar and restaurant meals; Car park (150); Witney 2 miles; ££££.

In the delectable countryside of the Upper Thames Valley and only two or three miles from the A40, this is a delightful Cotswold inn that makes a wonderful touring base with the dreaming spires of Oxford and the graceful grandeur of Blenheim Palace near at hand, to say nothing of a myriad enchanting Cotswold villages. This was originally a coaching house and farm which has been adapted to provide extremely comfortable cottage-style accommodation. Friendly and informal, the inn offers a high standard of cuisine, the à la carte menu in the restaurant emphasising fine English cooking. Wholesome fare in the form of home-made pies and farmhouse cheeses may also be enjoyed in the bar and lounges. 🌷🌷🌷 *Highly Commended, RAC***.*

THE MARLBOROUGH ARMS HOTEL,
Oxford Street, Woodstock,
Oxfordshire OX20 1TS

Tel: 01993 811227
Fax: 01993 811657

14 bedrooms, 12 with private bathroom; Free House with real ale; Historic interest; Bar and restaurant meals; Car park (30); Oxford 8 miles; ££££.

From its setting in the centre of the town in the shadow of Blenheim Palace, this fine old hotel adds much to the charm and sense of history of the ancient town of Woodstock, traditionally a haunt of the Angevin kings on their hunting trips in the New Forest. Now all guests, not just royal ones, are warmly welcomed by the friendly hosts and their efficient staff. With exposed oak beams and open fireplaces as traditional decorative features throughout combined with contemporary comforts, the Marlborough Arms offers the best of both worlds, both ancient and modern. Altogether a most civilised place to enjoy a drink and a snack, a meal, or an overnight stay.

NOTE

All the information in this book is given in good faith in the belief that it is correct. However, the publishers cannot guarantee the facts given in these pages, neither are they responsible for changes in policy, ownership or terms that may take place after the date of going to press. Readers should always satisfy themselves that the facilities they require are available and that the terms, if quoted, still apply.

Shropshire

TALBOT INN,
Much Wenlock,
Shropshire TF13 6AA

Tel: 01952 727077

6 bedrooms, all with private bathroom; Free House with real ale; Historic interest; Bar and restaurant meals; Car park (6); Bridgnorth 9 miles; £££.

Once part of Wenlock Abbey, this charming 13th century inn is entered through an archway which opens into a quiet courtyard garden; inside the exposed beams, open log fires and fresh flowers create a mood of relaxed contentment. Guest rooms with private facilities are in a converted malthouse in the courtyard, which also houses a comfortable residents' lounge and breakfast room; all are attractively furnished. A good choice of home-cooked dishes is available lunchtime and in the evening and even those on the strictest of diets should give in for once and sample the famous Bread and Butter Pudding, a speciality of the house. ☛ ☛ ☛ Commended, Egon Ronay Recommended.

THE LION,
Wyle Cop, Shrewsbury,
Shropshire SY1 1UY

Tel: 01743 353107
Fax: 01743 352744

59 bedrooms, all with private bathroom; Free House with real ale; Historic interest; Bar food, restaurant evenings only plus Sunday lunch; Car park (70); Birmingham 35 miles; ££££.

This imposing old inn has a long and fascinating history and several famous persons have crossed its threshold, including Charles Dickens after whom a spacious suite is named. Antiques and traditional furnishings highlight the inn's unique atmosphere, with pride of place going to the magnificent George III staircase which sweeps from ground floor to attic. Amenities are exactly of the standard one would expect of a first-class establishment, and the luxurious en suite bedrooms are fully equipped with everything for guests' comfort. Wining and dining here is a most pleasurable experience, with courteous and attentive service to make a stay, long or short, something to remember with satisfaction. ☛ ☛ ☛ ☛, AA and RAC ***.

Available from most bookshops, the 1995 edition of THE GOLF GUIDE covers details of every UK golf course – well over 2000 entries – for holiday or business golf. Hundreds of hotel entries offer convenient accommodation, accompanying details of the courses – the 'pro', par score, length etc.
Endorsed by The Professional Golfers' Association (PGA) and including Holiday Golf in Ireland, France, Portugal, Spain and the USA.
£8.50 from bookshops or £9.50 including postage (UK only) from FHG Publications, Abbey Mill Business Centre, Paisley PA1 1TJ.

Somerset

THE MALT SHOVEL INN,
Blackmoor Lane, Cannington, Bridgwater,
Somerset TA5 2NE
Tel: 01278 653432

4 bedrooms, one with private bathroom; Free House with real ale; Historic interest; Children welcome; Bar and restaurant meals; Car park; Taunton 9 miles.

Those who follow the Malt Shovel signpost near Cannington on the A39 west of Bridgwater will be amply rewarded. In addition to well-kept real ale and a most cheering welcome from licensees Robert and Frances Beverley they will find a tempting array of reasonably priced bar food, ranging from a freshly cut sandwich to more substantial homemade pies, and succulent fillet and sirloin steaks. Comfortable bed and breakfast accommodation is available, and residents who would dine in style are recommended to the very good restaurant which attracts both local and passing trade. Children are welcomed.

THE HORSE POND INN,
The Triangle, Castle Cary,
Somerset BA7 7BD
Tel: 01963 350318

4 motel rooms and 2 bedrooms, all en-suite; Free House with real ale; Historic interest; Children welcome; Bar and restaurant meals; Car park (20); Bournemouth 35 miles, Lyme Regis 32, Weymouth 30, Bristol 29, Weston-super-Mare 28, Bath 25.

This beautifully renovated old coaching inn dates back to the sixteenth century and today, under its welcoming hosts, Charlie and Fiona Anderson, specialises in good home cooking. In such a convivial atmosphere relaxation comes easily, with lively chatter with the locals and unspoilt countryside to walk and enjoy within a stone's throw from the inn. Castle Cary is delightfully placed for half-day visits to numerous places of geographic and historic interest, with day excursions including the coast which may be reached by car within one hour. The inn has very comfortably appointed accommodation and the terms represent excellent value, with reductions for a stay of one week or more. Six golf courses within half an hour's drive.

THE WALNUT TREE INN,
North Petherton, Bridgwater,
Somerset TA6 6QA
Tel: 01278 662255
Fax: 01278 663946

28 bedrooms, all with private bathroom; Free House with real ale; Historic interest; Children welcome; Bar and restaurant meals; Car park (72); Bridgwater 3 miles; £££.

In appearance a classic wayside hostelry, this delightfully renovated 18th century inn today has many of the attributes of a first-class hotel. One may still relax with a pint of real ale and rub shoulders with the locals in the bar and contemplate a menu offering excellent fare ranging from a well-filled granary roll to a succulent steak in the Cottage Room. For memorable à la carte dining, the tastefully decorated Sedgemoor Restaurant is justly popular and prices are very reasonable. Accommodation is of an extremely high standard, suiting the needs of holidaymakers and businessmen alike. Rooms, all en suite, are furnished in bright modern style and there are outstanding facilities for meetings and social events. ♥ ♥ ♥ ♥ *Commended, AA *** 70%, RAC ***, Egon Ronay, Ashley Courtenay.*

THE PECKING MILL INN,
Evercreech, Near Shepton Mallet,
Somerset BA4 6PG

Tel: 01749 830336
Fax: 01749 831316

6 bedrooms, all with private bathroom; Free House with real ale; Historic interest; Bar and restaurant meals; Car park (26); Shepton Mallet 4 miles; ££.

History, legend and breathtaking scenery combine in the Mendip area of Somerset to make it the perfect setting for a short break or longer stay, and at the Pecking Mill you will find added to these attractions warm hospitality and a friendly welcome for all. Bedrooms have everything one could wish for to make one's stay comfortable, including private bathrooms, colour television, direct-dial telephone, hairdryer and trouser press; the most attractive room rate includes a full English breakfast. The bar and restaurant retain the traditional atmosphere of the inn's 16th century origins and offer an excellent choice of good food, well kept ales and other refreshments. ♕♕♕, *AA**, RAC 2 Tankards.*

THE HATCH INN,
Hatch Beauchamp, Taunton,
Somerset TA3 6SG

Tel: 01823 480245

6 bedrooms; Free House with real ale; Children welcome; Bar and restaurant meals; Car park; Taunton 5 miles; £.

A friendly, family-owned and operated village inn, offering bed and breakfast; families catered for. All bedrooms have colour television and tea and coffee making facilities, and there is a pleasant dining room and a comfortable, well-stocked bar serving real ales. Home-cooked meals, including vegetarian dishes, are a speciality. The inn also has a very nice garden, a skittle alley, a spacious function room and a large car park. It is situated in a quiet village only a few minutes' drive from the M5 (Junction 25) and the county town of Taunton, amidst spectacular Somerset countryside. It makes a very good base for visiting the many attractions in South and West Somerset.

KINGS ARMS INN,
Montacute,
Somerset TA16 6UU

Tel: 01935 822513
Fax: 01935 826549

11 bedrooms, all with private bathroom; Free House with real ale; Historic interest; Bar food, restaurant evenings only; Car park; Yeovil 4 miles; £££.

The first acquaintance many people make with this welcoming and charismatic 16th century hamstone inn is after visiting nearby Elizabethan Montacute House. The atmosphere of the Pickwick Bar is typically that of a traditional English inn and in this happy setting, an extensive range of hot and cold buffet dishes and snacks is served. Each evening the Abbey Room Restaurant presents a splendid selection of à la carte dishes. Now blessed with impressive hotel amenities, the Kings Arms has a number of beautifully decorated guest rooms, including a four-poster room and a half-tester room, all of which have a private bathroom, colour television, radio and tea and coffee-making facilities. ♛ ♛ ♛ ♛ *Highly Commended.*

MANOR ARMS,
North Perrott,
Somerset TA18 7SG

Tel: 01460 72901

5 bedrooms, all with private bathroom; Free House with real ale; Historic interest; Children welcome; Bar and restaurant meals; Car park (26); Crewkerne 2 miles; ££.

A focal point of a village of lovely hamstone cottages, this handsome 16th century Grade II listed building displays abundant character through its exposed stonework, inglenook fireplace and original oak beams, the bar warmed by a log fire in cool weather. Lovingly restored and having acquired a reputation for its superb (and reasonably-priced) English fare, this typical wayside inn overlooks the green. This is a tranquil area of picture-book villages and verdant, undulating countryside with the Dorset coast within 20 minutes' drive and a number of historic houses close at hand. Five charming, comfortable bedrooms, all en suite, are situated in the adjacent coach house, the ideal venue for a quiet and rewarding break. ♛ ♛ *Commended, AA QQQ.*

THE FULL MOON AT RUDGE,
Near Bath,
Somerset BA11 2QG

Tel: 01373 830936
Fax: 01373 831366

5 bedrooms, all with private bathroom; Free House with real ale; Historic interest; Children welcome; Bar and restaurant meals (Sunday carvery lunchtimes only); Car park; Bath 10 miles, Longleat 4; £££.

This award-winning 17th century country inn lies just off the A36 in the small hamlet of Rudge, where the owners Patrick and Christine Gifford have established high standards of personal service and traditional hospitality. Their real ales are featured by CAMRA, while the superb food makes eating here a memorable, but not expensive, occasion. The comfortable en suite bedrooms, all with direct-dial telephones, television and tea/coffee making facilities, overlook the extensive gardens, and all have a panoramic view of the Westbury White Horse. Central to the towns of Trowbridge, Westbury, Frome and Warminster and only 10 miles from Bath, The Full Moon is the ideal touring centre for the area.

THE CARPENTERS ARMS,
Stanton Wick, Near Pensford,
Somerset BS18 4BX

Tel: 01761 490202
Fax: 01761 490763

12 bedrooms, all with private bathroom; Free House with real ale; Bar and restaurant meals; Car park; Chew Magna 3 miles; ££££.

A very civilised establishment, where standards of service and cuisine will satisfy the most discerning, yet where genuine friendliness and courtesy are as natural and refreshing as the clean country air. Converted from a row of old miners' cottages, this is everyone's picture of a real country inn. The beamed restaurant is a stylish and relaxing setting for the enjoyment of imaginative, freshly prepared food, including daily delivered seafood; alternatively, light meals and snacks as well as traditional pub favourites can be taken in the Coopers Parlour. Good wines are something of a speciality here (in particular some fine clarets). If in need of overnight accommodation, 12 delightful en suite bedrooms may provide the solution, especially if you can take advantage of the special weekend break rates.

WINCHESTER ARMS,
Church Road, Trull, Taunton,
Somerset TA3 7LG

Tel: 01823 284723

4 bedrooms; Free House with real ale; Historic interest; Children welcome; Bar and restaurant meals; Car park; Taunton 2 miles.

Most competently run by the hospitable licensees, this white-washed hostelry enjoys the peaceful rural setting of Trull village, just one and a half miles south of Taunton and a recommended touring base. Overnight guests are offered comfortable, prettily furnished bedrooms which retain old-world appeal while having modern facilities such as colour television and tea/coffee makers, and a full English breakfast is included in the accommodation charge. Dinner is served in the attractively decorated restaurant, where the finest of local produce is presented in a highly professional manner. A good range of beers, wines, spirits (and conversation) will be found in the locally popular bar.

RALEGH'S CROSS INN,
Brendon Hills, Near Watchet,
Somerset TA23 0LN   Tel: 01984 640343

9 bedrooms, all with private bathroom; Free House; Historic interest; Bar and restaurant meals; Car park (200); Minehead 15 miles, Barnstaple 15, Exford 13.

The gateway to Exmoor, 1250 feet above sea level in an area of outstanding natural beauty, this comfortable old inn set in its own large grounds offers ground floor and first floor tastefully decorated en suite rooms with colour television. An extensive menu with freshly prepared starters, over 25 main courses and desserts to suit all tastes can be enjoyed in the large bar area with cosy log fires and a newly found well, or in the restaurant. Families welcome in our attractive family dining room, also rustic play area.

THE REST AND BE THANKFUL INN,
Wheddon Cross, Near Minehead,
Somerset TA24 7DR   Tel and Fax: 01643 841222

4 bedrooms, all with private bathroom; Free House with real ales; Historic interest; Children welcome; Bar and restaurant meals; Car park; Dunster 5 miles; ££.

After an exhilarating day exploring the wild and picturesque moorland, one's first thought on catching sight of this neat cream-painted inn must surely be "what an appropriate name!". Rest is assured in the comfortable, well-appointed bedrooms, each with en suite shower and enjoying sweeping views of Dunkery Beacon, the highest point in Somerset. The hungry or thirsty traveller will be thankful too for the traditional home-cooked meals and snacks served in the restaurant and bar, accompanied perhaps by a glass of well kept ale or a selection from the carefully chosen wine list. In finer weather patrons can relax in the charming garden patio, while the more actively inclined can make use of the games room and skittle alley. 🌸 🌸 🌸 *Highly Commended, RAC, Les Routiers.*

SQUIRREL INN,
Laymore, Winsham, Chard,
Somerset TA20 4NT
Tel: 0146-030 298

3 bedrooms, all with shower rooms; Free House with real ale; Children welcome; Bar food; Car park (30); Chard 4 miles; ££.

Limited but singularly comfortable accommodation is on hand at this nice little country pub, and all guest rooms have the welcome facilities of en suite shower and toilet, colour television, central heating and tea trays. Bar food is offered seven days a week and a range of home-made specials supplement a good and varied regular menu. Children are greeted with a smile here, and a family room is available together with a safe, well-equipped play area in the inn's extensive gardens. Real ale is served with friendly courtesy, and farmhouse cider provides a challenge to the daring.

Staffordshire

BLACK LION INN,
Butterton, Near Leek,
Staffordshire ST13 7ST
Tel: 01538 304232

3 bedrooms, all with private bathroom; Free House with real ale; Historic interest; Children welcome; Bar food, restaurant weekends only; Car park (60); Leek 6 miles; ££.

With magnificent views over the Peak District National Park and only a mile from the scenic Manifold Valley, this traditional country inn, a Listed building, is unsophisticated and friendly, treasuring true hospitality high amongst the worthwhile things of life. The inn has abundant character evidenced in its exposed beams, stone walls and open fires. The bars have several alcoves and rooms leading off and the walls are festooned with brass, china, pictures and whisky jugs. English cuisine of high merit is offered in the recently opened Roasterie Carvery Restaurant and dining room; there is also a varied bar snack menu. Attractive and comfortable accommodation is available at remarkably reasonable rates. *ETB* 👥 👥 👥, *Good Pub Guide.*

THREE HORSESHOES INN,
Blackshaw Moor, Leek,
Staffordshire ST13 8TW

Tel: 01538 300296
Fax: 01538 300320

6 bedrooms, all with private shower; Free House with real ale; Children welcome; Bar and restaurant meals; Car park (100); Derby 28 miles, Stafford 24, Stoke-on-Trent 11, Buxton 7; ££.

This family-run inn is situated on the A53, approximately seven miles from Buxton, with breathtaking views of the Staffordshire Moorlands and the bizarre stone formation of The Roaches. Stone walls, oak beams and log fires give an olde worlde atmosphere. Fine traditional foods are served in the Carvery, while the restaurant offers à la carte and candlelit menus using fresh vegetables and local beef, poultry, game and cheeses, accompanied by a fine wine list. At weekends a well-attended dinner dance offers a fine choice of food, wine, music and dancing into the early hours. Accommodation is available in six cottage-style bedrooms, with showers, telephone, television and tea-making facilities. For relaxation in fine weather there are large gardens with patios, terraces and a children's play area. *ETB* 👑👑 *Commended, Logis, Les Routiers, Egon Ronay Recommended.*

Key to
Tourist Board Ratings

The Crown Scheme
(England, Scotland & Wales)

Covering hotels, motels, private hotels, guesthouses, inns, bed & breakfast, farmhouses. Every Crown classified place to stay is inspected annually. *The classification:* Listed then 1-5 Crown indicates the range of facilities and services. Higher quality standards are indicated by the terms APPROVED, COMMENDED, HIGHLY COMMENDED and DELUXE.

The Key Scheme
(also operates in Scotland using a Crown symbol)

Covering self-catering in cottages, bungalows, flats, houseboats, houses, chalets, etc. Every Key classified holiday home is inspected annually. *The classification:* 1-5 Key indicates the range of facilities and equipment. Higher quality standards are indicated by the terms APPROVED, COMMENDED, HIGHLY COMMENDED and DELUXE.

The Q Scheme
(England, Scotland & Wales)

Covering holiday, caravan, chalet and camping parks. Every Q rated park is inspected annually for its quality standards. The more √ in the Q – up to 5 – the higher the standard of what is provided.

Suffolk

THE SIX BELLS COUNTRY INN,
The Green, Bardwell, Bury St. Edmunds,
Suffolk IP31 1AW
Tel: 01359 250820

8 bedrooms, all with private shower; Free House with real ale; Historic interest; Children welcome; Bar and restaurant meals; Car park (40); Ixworth 2 miles; ££/£££.

We can but add our accolade to many accorded to this attractive, 16th century inn, run superbly by Carol and Richard Salmon. Peace, comfort and good living are the rewards of a visit to this refreshing backwater in the turbulent tide of life. Conversion of the old barn and stables have provided beautifully furnished rooms, all of which are at ground-floor level. Each has a shower en suite, colour television, tea and coffee-makers and controlled heating. Imaginative meals of high quality are served in both bar and charming restaurant — Salmon Trout in Champagne Sauce; Spinach and Cream Cheese Pancakes — we could go on but space precludes. All the delights of a country free house are here — good food and drink in a friendly and hospitable atmosphere. ♣♣♣ *Commended, AA QQQQ Selected, Les Routiers Pub of the Year 1993, Corps d'Elite Wine Award 1993/1994, Casserole Award.*

ANGEL INN,
Stoke-by-Nayland, Near Colchester,
Suffolk CO6 4SA
Tel: 01206 263245

6 bedrooms, all with private bathroom; Free House with real ale; Historic interest; Bar and restaurant meals, lunch and evening; Car park (25); Hadleigh 5 miles; ££££.

Advice to make a prior booking shows the local popularity enjoyed by the Angel's restaurant — but if one has omitted to do so and is denied the delights of the à la carte dinner menu, all is not lost. Meals on offer in the homely bar prove a worthy alternative and are exceedingly good value as well as being wholesome, satisfying and well presented. Those seeking accommodation in Constable country will be well pleased with what is on offer at this sixteenth-century village inn. En suite guest bedrooms are both attractive and comfortable, and colour television, tea and coffee facilities and telephone are provided in all. ♣♣♣ *Commended.*

Surrey

ANCHOR HOTEL,
Church Square, Shepperton-on-Thames, Surrey TW17 9JY

Tel: 01932 221618
Fax: 01932 252235

29 bedrooms, all with private bathroom; Free House with real ale; Historic interest; Bar food, restaurant evenings only; Car park (20); London 15 miles; ££££.

One of our most famous and traditional inns, this fascinating hostelry has opened its great oak doors to welcome guests for 400 years and has played host to such guests as Charles Dickens (in memory of whom a room is named), Lord Nelson, Sir William Hamilton, Dick Turpin (who slept in the little room in the roof) and the poets, Peacock and Byron; in more recent years, Elizabeth Taylor and Richard Burton stayed here during the filming of "Beckett". Amongst whispered tales of romance, chivalry and violent crime, guests are invited to relax today in these unrushed surroundings and ponder on the visitors of bygone days. The Anchor still retains its old-world charm serving real ale and a large selection of other beers and lagers and the wine bar is a popular meeting place, whilst dining here in such a relaxed atmosphere is a joy of its own. A tempting range of bar meals is on offer every lunchtime and in the evening. First-class and admirably modernised accommodation is available in the form of bedrooms with en suite facilities, colour television, direct-dial telephone and tea and coffee-makers. As the inn's impressive brochure states: "Through the portals of this Inn have passed the Rich, the Famous, Prime Ministers, Statesmen, Pugilists, Notorious Personages of Dubious Character, Wenches, Visitors from the Colonies (including the Americas), Sporting Gentry, Vagabonds, Glamorous Artists from the World of Motion Pictures, but the most important of all is You!" *Egon Ronay Recommended.*

The **£** symbol when appearing at the end of the italic section of an entry shows the anticipated price, during 1995, for **single full Bed and Breakfast.**

Under £30	£	Over £45 but under £60	£££
Over £30 but under £45	££	Over £60	££££

This is meant as an indication only and does not show prices for Special Breaks, Weekends, etc. Guests are therefore advised to verify all prices on enquiring or booking.

East Sussex

THE GRIFFIN INN,
Fletching, Near Uckfield,
East Sussex TN22 3SS

Tel: 01825 722890

4 bedrooms, all with private bathroom; Free House with real ale; Historic interest; Children welcome; Bar and restaurant meals; Car park (30); Uckfield 3 miles; ££/£££.

It is hard to imagine a more delightful setting than that of this long, low 16th century inn. Wander into the garden and the beauty of the South Downs is spread before you; almost next door is the National Trust property of Sheffield Park whose beautifully landscaped gardens and lakes were laid out by Capability Brown. Inside, oak beams, gleaming copper and open fireplaces create a most relaxing setting for the enjoyment of the imaginative home-prepared bar and restaurant meals, particularly so on one of the regular gourmet evenings which are such a popular feature. If tempted to linger awhile in this most tranquil spot, traditionally styled bedrooms, some with four-posters, can be obtained at most reasonable rates. 🌢🌢, *Egon Ronay "Wine Pub of the Year" 1992, "Sussex Dining Out Pub of the Year" 1994.*

BEST BEECH INN,
Mayfield Lane, Wadhurst,
East Sussex TN5 6JH

Tel: 01892 782046
Fax: 01892 785092

7 bedrooms, 4 with private bathroom; Free House with real ale; Historic interest; Bar and restaurant meals (not Sun./Mon.); Car park; Tunbridge Wells 6 miles; ££.

Close to the Kent and Sussex border, this most attractive hostelry dates back, in part, to 1680 although it is largely Victorian in character. Recently refurbished in style, without disturbing its period appeal, the inn is surrounded by lush Wealden countryside and is within one hour's drive of London and the coast. Known for its excellent food, either in the fine restaurant or friendly bar, this is a recommended port of call for refreshment. By reason of its happy location with many historic buildings in the area, many enlightened guests make this a residential base for touring. Many of the comfortable bedrooms have en suite facilities and all have television and tea and coffee-makers.

West Sussex

GUN INN,
High Street, Findon, Worthing,
West Sussex BN14 0TA

Tel: 01903 873206

No accommodation; Whitbread House with real ale; Historic interest; Bar and restaurant meals; Car park (31); Worthing 4 miles.

In a beautiful situation surrounded by woods and rolling hills, Findon is a charming and unspoilt downland village. We found the Gun to be a homely and welcoming port of call; nothing fancy but just good old traditional worth. It dates from the 16th century and the low-beamed lounge bar contains beams that were once timbers of old ships. There is a fine selection of real ales and wholesome cooked food is served at lunchtime and on most evenings. The sea is within easy reach and nearby is the great earthwork of Cissbury Ring (N.T.) which rises 600 feet above sea level. Josh Gifford's racing stables are nearby and, straight from the horse's mouth, this friendly inn is certainly well worth a visit.

SWAN INN,
Lower Street, Fittleworth, Near Pulborough,
West Sussex RH20 1EN

Tel: 01798 865429
Fax: 01798 865546

10 bedrooms, 8 with private bathroom; Whitbread House with real ale; Historic interest; Children welcome; Bar and restaurant meals; Car park (20); Petworth 3 miles; £££.

Nestling in the verdant Sussex countryside, we found this attractive old 14th century inn on the A283 between Petworth and Pulborough a cheering sight, a promise fulfilled by early acquaintance with the refreshment available in its friendly bars. There is also a first-class à la carte restaurant where the menu offers an exciting choice of dishes. As a base for wandering free over the South Downs or when visiting Glorious Goodwood for the races, this delightful hostelry has much to commend it. Terms for excellent en suite accommodation represent good value and include a full English breakfast. Some rooms have four-poster beds. *SETB* ⚘ ⚘ ⚘, *AA and RAC***.

FORESTERS ARMS,
Kirdford, Billingshurst,
West Sussex RH14 0ND

Tel: 01403 820205

3 bedrooms; King & Barnes House with real ale; Historic interest; Bar food, restaurant evenings only (not Tuesday); Car park; Petworth 4 miles.

Alongside the green of a charming West Sussex village, we judge this picturesque 15th century inn to be the stuff of which dreams of "Our England" are made. The hostelry itself consists of a comfortable saloon bar and a public bar with large inglenook fireplace and polished stone-flagged floor; here, such traditional games as crib, dominoes, skittles and darts may be played. An appetising variety of hot and cold home-cooked lunches are available daily. First-rate, freshly cooked evening meals are served in an attractive country-style restaurant every night except Tuesday, the menu being changed weekly. We also do sheep and hog roasts in winter, and live music nights (jazz, folk and country groups), are a feature. Guests may book overnight accommodation in clean, well-appointed rooms at very reasonable rates.

THE SUSSEX PAD,
Lancing,
West Sussex BN15 0RH

Tel: 01273 454647
Fax: 01273 453010

18 bedrooms, all with private bathroom; Free House with real ale; Historic interest; Bar and restaurant meals; Car park; Worthing 2 miles; ££££.

Refreshingly furnished and decorated in modern mode, this delightful inn/hotel proves that it is possible to be colourful in cheerful contemporary style and tasteful at the same time. In the shadow of Lancing College's dominant structure and but a mile from the seafront, the present Sussex Pad has a luxurious lounge bar, a favourite meeting place prior, possibly, to adjourning to the spruce Ladywell's Restaurant which sports a comprehensive menu. The preparation and presentation of dishes is of the highest standard with an intriguing selection of wines from around the world in attendance. Honeyman's Outlook, the imposing south-facing conservatory, is air-conditioned and takes its name from a freshwater spring used over the centuries by thirsty travellers; from here there are panoramic views of the Adur Valley and Shoreham Airport. The original inn, dating back to the 15th century, was a favourite haunt of smugglers because of its lonely position near the river and its cellars were very convenient for storing contraband. It was destroyed by fire in 1905. Today, the hostelry presents superb accommodation in the form of executive rooms all with showers and baths with Victorian gold-plated fittings, satellite television, radio, direct-dial telephone, shaver points, hair dryer, trouser press, tea and coffee-making facilities and individually-controlled central heating. There are also four-poster suites, ideal for honeymoons or that romantic weekend. Children of all ages are welcome and subject to certain reductions. 🍸🍸🍸🍸 *Commended, AA Rosette.*

Warwickshire

HALFORD BRIDGE INN,
Fosseway, Halford, Shipston-on-Stour,
Warwickshire CV36 5BN
Tel: 01789 740382

6 bedrooms, 3 with showers; Free House; Historic interest; Bar and restaurant meals; Car park (40); NEC and Airport 25 miles, Banbury 12, Stratford-upon-Avon 8; M40 (Junction 12) 7.

On the principle that you can't have too much of a good thing Tony and Greta Westwood, proprietors of this charming sixteenth century inn, keep their kitchens open seven days a week to provide sustenance to regulars, residents and hungry passers-by. A wide range of good hot and cold bar food is available, in addition to the excellent fare offered at reasonable prices in the restaurant. Good home cooking is the speciality here, with home-made pickles, sauces, pies etc, as well as fresh vegetables whenever possible. All the comfortably furnished bedrooms have colour television, and tourists who must keep an eye on their budgets as well as the scenery will find them good value for money. *ETB* ♛♛*, Les Routiers, AA Recommended, CAMRA.*

HOWARD ARMS,
Lower Green, Ilmington, Near Shipston-on-Stour,
Warwickshire CV36 4LN
Tel and Fax: 01608 682226

2 bedrooms, both with private bathroom; Free House with real ale; Historic interest; Children welcome; Bar and restaurant meals; Car park (33); Shipston-on-Stour 4 miles; £££.

The delightful bar with heavy oak beams, flagstone floor and open fireplaces, betrays the 17th century origins of the Howard Arms. On the village green of a pretty Cotswold village of honey-stone cottages and within easy reach of Stratford-upon-Avon, the inn is increasingly popular with tourists seeking good food and drink in a tranquil atmosphere. Prices are reasonable and vegetarian fare is available. A 55-seater restaurant is provided in addition to accommodation in the form of a twin-bedded room and a king-size bedded room, both with full en suite facilities, colour television, hair dryers and tea and coffee-makers. Outside is an attractive garden with tables and chairs where families may refresh themselves in the summer. ♛♛ *Commended, Les Routiers, Egon Ronay.*

WHITE HORSE INN,
Banbury Road, Ettington, Near Stratford-upon-Avon,
Warwickshire CV37 7SU
Tel: 01789 740641

4 bedrooms, all en-suite; Real ale; Historic interest; Bar and restaurant meals; Car park (30); Oxford 34 miles, Birmingham 30, Stratford-upon-Avon 6; ££££ (double room).

What could be more delightful for a holiday or short break in Shakespeare country than a stop-over in this lovely old inn, already conjuring up the atmosphere of days gone by with its furnishings, oak beams, and the warmth of its welcome. Guests can enjoy a glass of real ale with their lunch, and for those who choose to stay longer, the Inn's restaurant serves fine fare in the evening. There is a sun patio and beer garden in which to take advantage of warmer weather. The White Horse's accommodation means that tired visitors may take full advantage of its location, six miles from Stratford and close to Warwick Castle and the Cotswolds. Also near to NEC Birmingham and the Royal Showground at Stoneleigh. All rooms are tastefully furnished and en suite, with colour television, central heating and tea/coffee making facilities. Weekend break reductions from November to April. Proprietors Roy and Val Blower. *ETB* ♨♨.

KING'S HEAD HOTEL,
Warwick Road, Wellesbourne,
Warwickshire CV35 9LX   Tel: 01789 840206

9 bedrooms, all with private bathroom; Bass House with real ale; Historic interest; Children welcome; Bar and restaurant meals; Car park (40); Stratford-upon-Avon 6 miles, Warwick 7 miles; £££.

Cosy and intimate in atmosphere, The King's Head has nine bedrooms, each furnished in pleasing "country cottage" style, with television, radio, and tea/coffee making facilities. Children are welcome, and parents will appreciate the spacious family rooms which are available. The open plan restaurant provides the perfect setting for freshly prepared and imaginative menus, combining the quality of a superior restaurant with the informality of a pub. Set in beautiful countryside, yet with easy motorway connections to the M40, M42 and M6, this is an ideal choice whether on business or pleasure.

Wiltshire

RED LION INN,
Axford, Near Marlborough,
Wiltshire SN8 2HA   Tel: 01672 520271

4 bedrooms, all with private bathroom; Free House with real ale; Children welcome; Bar and restaurant meals; Car park (30); Marlborough 3 miles; ££.

Specialising in fish and seafood with game in season, this homely flint and brick hostelry lies in the lush Kennet Valley on the very banks of the River Kennet. Just to the north of the Savernake Forest, this is lovely undulating countryside with the racecourse training centres of Lambourn and Beckhampton, Avebury Stone Circles and numerous pretty villages in the vicinity. Guests may be assured of a friendly welcome from Hosts, Daphne and Mel Evans, who preside over the excellent à la carte and bar food dishes, the restaurant being thoughtfully divided into separate smoking and non-smoking sections. Taking refreshment in the beer garden is a relaxing pastime in clement weather. A delightful spot for a quiet holiday, the inn boasts first-rate en suite accommodation. 👙 👙, *Egon Ronay.*

BIDDESTONE ARMS,
Biddestone, Near Chippenham,
Wiltshire SN14 7DC
Tel: 01249 714377

No accommodation; Free House with real ale; Historic interest; Children welcome; Bar and restaurant meals; Car park; Chippenham 4 miles.

The friendly proprietors are on hand to bid a welcome to all patrons of this nice little stone pub which stands at one end of the quiet Wiltshire village of Biddestone. The Biddestone Arms is a free house and offers a fine selection of well-kept real ales and other refreshments, and food menus ranging from snacks to full sit-down meals are also available. This is a good place to stop for a traditional Sunday lunch, or perhaps when on a day out to nearby Castle Combe Motor Racing Circuit. In warmer weather visitors may take their ease in the pub's pleasant garden.

QUEEN'S HEAD,
Broad Chalke, Near Salisbury,
Wiltshire SP5 5EN
Tel: 01722 780344

4 bedrooms, all with private bathroom; Free House with real ale; Historic interest; Bar and restaurant meals; Car park (40); Bournemouth 30 miles, Salisbury 7; ££

Just seven miles from Salisbury yet in a lovely rural setting, the old world charm of this inn has been in no way marred by its careful upgrading. En suite guest rooms are spacious and well designed, and each is equipped with colour television, tea-making facilities and telephone. A comprehensive menu operates throughout the inn plus daily "specials". The quality and variety of the food offered is excellent and you can take your meal in the quaintly traditional bar or in one of the separate dining lounges, one of which is non-smoking. The inn is personally run by Bernard and Pamela Lott. *WCTB* ♥ ♥ ♥, *CAMRA National Good Pub Guide Listed.*

THE COMPASSES INN,
Chicksgrove, Tisbury, Near Salisbury,
Wiltshire SP3 6NB
Tel and Fax: 01722 714318; Mobile: 0585 407191

3 bedrooms, 2 with private bathroom; Free House with real ale; Historic interest; Children welcome; Bar and restaurant meals; Car park (25); Salisbury 11 miles, Tisbury 2; ££.

If a visit to the historic city of Salisbury is on your itinerary, then make a slight detour to the pretty village of Chicksgrove where this Grade II Listed thatched freehouse provides rest and refreshment. The inn's history can be traced as far back as the 14th century, and while facilities have been brought right up-to-date, traditional furnishings and good old-fashioned hospitality remind one of a more leisurely age. A fine selection of ales, wines and spirits are the perfect accompaniment to one's choice from the tasty and nutritious menus available at lunchtime and in the evenings. Bed and breakfast accommodation is available at rates guaranteed to keep one's bank manager happy. *Egon Ronay.*

SOMERSET ARMS,
Church Street, Maiden Bradley,
Wiltshire BA12 7HW
Tel: 01985 844207

3 bedrooms; Wadworth House with real ale; Historic interest; Children welcome; Bar meals; Car park (25); Frome, Mere, Warminster and Bruton all 6 miles; £.

Built by the Duke of Somerset as a guest lodge, the Somerset Arms is now a friendly village inn serving Wadworth real ales and home-cooked country food. The pretty garden and barbecue are popular in summer, and in winter open fires in both bars make it a cosy haven. Pub games such as pool, skittles, darts and shove ha'penny are popular in the Public Bar. There are three large bedrooms. There is good walking country all around; Stourhead Gardens and Longleat are both close by, and within an hour are the cities of Bath, Bristol, Salisbury and Wells, and many National Trust properties and other places of interest.

THE OLD MILL AT HARNHAM,
Town Path, Salisbury,
Wiltshire SP2 8EU

Tel: 01722 322364
Fax: 01722 333367

11 bedrooms, all with private bathroom; Free House with real ale; Historic interest; Children welcome; Bar and restaurant meals; Car park (20); Southampton 21 miles; £££.

With delightful riverside gardens, this tranquil hostelry has immense character and an interesting history. It originates from the early 18th century when it was built as a warehouse attached to an ancient papermaking mill with three water wheels taking water from the River Nadder. The three races can be seen today coursing through the restaurant, the setting for the presentation of superb meals in the distinctive English tradition. Snacks, real ales and malt whiskies are served in a typical country pub bar. Salisbury is conveniently near and, indeed, there are fine views of the cathedral from the inn. A peaceful and rewarding place in which to stay, the Old Mill has excellently appointed bedrooms, all with private bathrooms. 👑 👑 👑 *Commended.*

Worcestershire

THE GREEN DRAGON,
Bishop's Frome,
Worcestershire WR6 5BP

Tel: 01885 490607

No accommodation; Free House with real ale; Historic interest; Children welcome; Bar and restaurant meals; Car park; Bromyard 4 miles.

This traditional English inn is a real find for beer buffs with its wide choice of ales regularly available, including a number of guest brews. All may be enjoyed in delightful surroundings, both indoor and out. The old bar, with its great open fireplace, stone floors and beamed ceiling, provides an idyllic setting for such sampling, or perhaps in company with a good meal served in an adjacent dining room. Summer days see the garden filled with family parties taking refreshment on the large lawn. This is a safe area for children for whom a swing and climbing frame are provided.

THE FLEECE,
Bretforton, Near Evesham,
Worcestershire WR11 5JE
Tel: 01386 831173

No accommodation; Free House with real ale; Historic interest; Children welcome; Bar food (not Monday evenings); Evesham 4 miles.

A visit to this charming hostelry is absolutely essential for all those who are interested in social history, for it is no exaggeration to say that The Fleece is a living museum. Committed to the care of the National Trust by a redoubtable lady, Miss Lola Taplin, whose family owned the building for centuries, it has been preserved much as it was on her death in 1977 — even her ornaments and furniture are still in their original places! The Fleece is therefore a genuine old country pub, and in the fine tradition of the country hostelry offers a superb range of hot and cold meals and snacks, good quality wines and beers, and, of course, a truly warm welcome. There is a large garden with a play area for children.

CHEQUERS INN,
Chequers Lane, Fladbury, Pershore,
Worcestershire WR10 2PZ
Tel: 01386 860276

8 bedrooms, all with private bathroom; Free House with real ale; Historic interest; Bar and restaurant meals; Car park (25); Evesham 3 miles.

A perfect example of the traditional English hostelry, the Chequers Inn stands at the end of a quiet lane in this delightful village in the Vale of Evesham. Those seeking accommodation will find beautifully kept en suite guest rooms, individually furnished and decorated, some with balconies, some with open rural views, and all well equipped with every modern facility, including television, radio, telephone and tea trays. Even if time precludes one staying a while in this charmed area, the Chequers is still worth a flying visit for its fine fare. A carvery is provided Thursday, Friday and Saturday evenings and Sunday lunchtime, while bar meals and an à la carte menu are available daily except on Sunday evening when it is residents only. *ETB* 🌑🌑🌑 *Commended.*

THE HADLEY BOWLING GREEN INN,
Hadley Heath, Near Droitwich,
Worcestershire WR9 0AR
Tel: 01905 620294
Fax: 01905 620771

14 bedrooms, all with private bathroom; Free House with real ale; Historic interest; Dinners and snacks; Car park (80); Worcester 5 miles, Droitwich 3; ££££.

This historic 16th century inn is situated in the heart of Worcestershire, yet only 10 minutes from the M5 motorway. The bowling green itself is one of the oldest in Britain, and was played on by many of the leading Elizabethan nobility. All bedrooms have private bath/shower and toilet, colour television, direct-dial telephone, hairdryer, trouser press and tea/coffee making facilities. Some have four-posters; three cottage-style rooms across the courtyard are ideal for those who prefer ground floor accommodation. An extensive à la carte menu is offered and a comprehensive bar snack menu is available in the three delightful bars, which also feature a wide choice of beers. This friendly, relaxed inn is convenient for Worcester and Droitwich and only 30 minutes' drive from the NEC and Birmingham Airport. *ETB* 🌑🌑🌑 *Commended, Logis, Les Routiers.*

North Yorkshire

"THE INN ON THE RIVER"

SHIP INN,
Acaster Malbis, York,
North Yorkshire YO2 1VH

Tel: 01904 705609/703888
Fax: 01904 705971

8 bedrooms, all with private facilities; Free House with real ale; Historic interest; Children welcome; Bar and restaurant meals; Car park (50); Leeds 17 miles, York 3; £££.

This attractive and well-run hostelry on the banks of the Ouse is only a short distance from the magnificence of York, the United Kingdom's second most popular tourist attraction. Offering first-class fare and spruce accommodation, including one four-poster bedroom and a family room, the inn makes a superb holiday headquarters and is equally popular with boating enthusiasts and businessmen. Excellent evening dinners are served in the relaxed atmosphere of the restaurant, whilst a wide range of lunches and evening snacks may be enjoyed in the friendly Riverside Bar. The inn now boasts a conservatory with water fountains, tropical plants and river views and has its own moorings for residents and visitors, as well as fishing rights. Further afield, the Yorkshire Dales beckon and the coast may be reached in less than an hour. *Tourist Board Listed "Commended", AA Listed.*

RED LION HOTEL,
Burnsall, Near Skipton,
North Yorkshire BD23 6BU

Tel: 01756 720204
Fax: 01756 720292

11 bedrooms, all with private bathroom; Free House with real ale; Historic interest; Children welcome; Bar and restaurant meals; Car park (70); Ilkley 12 miles, Skipton 9; £££.

This lovely old country village hotel, which was originally a sixteenth-century ferryman's inn, is situated on the banks of the River Wharfe. Seven miles of trout and grayling fishing are available on the river. We offer superb food, fine wines and real ale in the most wonderful of surroundings. Our award-winning chef, James Rowley, and his kitchen team serve a wide variety of bar food both lunchtimes and evenings. Our restaurant is open each evening and also for traditional Sunday lunch. All our food is freshly prepared daily, using a wide variety of specialised local produce. With food ranging from traditional steak and kidney pie, home-cured gravadlax of salmon, locally smoked duck and chicken to sticky toffee pudding, there is something for everyone at the Red Lion. With accommodation in the most relaxing of atmospheres, you can be assured of a warm welcome here. ♥ ♥ ♥ *Highly Commended, AA and RAC**, Ashley Courtenay Recommended.*

THE TRADDOCK HOTEL,
Austwick, Near Settle,
North Yorkshire LA2 8BY

Tel and Fax: 015242 51224

11 bedrooms, all with private bathroom; Free House; Historic interest; Children welcome; Bar and restaurant meals; Car park (22); Settle 4 miles; £££.

A real Yorkshire welcome, delectable food and an exciting variety of ways to work up an appetite can be the rewards of a holiday spent at the Traddock, where hosts, Frances and Richard Michaelis, are well versed in the arts of guest care. In a picturesque, dramatic and unspoilt setting in the Yorkshire Dales National Park, this superbly run hostelry exudes charm and character, as epitomised in its cosy bar and lounges with open fires to warm the cockles of the heart. "Relax and be spoilt" — a motto that sums up the friendly service here. Start the day with a hearty breakfast while you plan the day's activities — an achievement in itself as there is so much to see and do in the area. One's return later will be full of mouthwatering anticipation of the appetising, varied dishes and convivial company that may be enjoyed in the evening, and then, all too soon, off to restful repose in a magnificently appointed en suite room with colour television, direct-dial telephone, electric blankets, and tea and coffee making facilities and dream of the morrow. There is a Falconry Centre and two spectacular caves nearby, and the Lake District and coast are also easily reached. Golf, fishing and pony trekking are available in the area. This is a highly regarded Yorkshire gem. ♕♕♕ *Commended, AA/RAC **, Les Routiers.*

SHIP INN,
Low Road, Aldborough, Near Boroughbridge,
North Yorkshire YO5 9ER
Tel: 01423 322749

4 bedrooms, all with private bathroom; Free House with real ale; Historic interest; Bar food, restaurant evenings only; Car park; Ripon 7 miles, Knaresborough 6; ££.

Only a mile from the A1, Aldborough is a typical English village with a green, maypole and stocks. The Ship's two comfortable bars are a focal point for the social life of the village, the carefully preserved charm of this 14th century inn reflecting the ambience of a bygone era through its log fires, exposed timbers and traditional pub furnishings. Home-made meals and snacks are served at lunchtime and in the evening; there is also an à la carte restaurant in the evening. Furnished in modern style, bedrooms have en suite facilities, colour television and tea and coffee-makers.

THE FORESTERS ARMS,
Carlton-in-Coverdale, Near Leyburn,
North Yorkshire DL8 2BB
Tel: 01969 40272

3 bedrooms, all with private bathroom; Free House with real ale; Historic interest; Children welcome; Bar and restaurant meals; Car park; Wensley 4 miles; ££.

In a picturesque village in the heart of the Yorkshire Dales National Park, the Foresters Arms has been dispensing good cheer and refreshment since the seventeenth century. Beautifully refurbished, its bars retain a warm and friendly atmosphere aided by the visual assurance of open log fires and beamed ceilings. A selection of cask-conditioned Yorkshire ales will also contribute to a relaxed and happy mood in company with first-rate bar meals. One may also dine sumptuously and inexpensively in the well regarded restaurant, where the menus feature the finest of local produce. This is a lovely place in which to stay, and admirable accommodation is available in stylishly appointed bedrooms with en suite facilities. 🌷 🌷 🌷 *Highly Commended, AA QQQ, RAC Acclaimed, Egon Ronay, Good Food Guide, Good Pub Guide.*

NEW INN,
Clapham, Near Settle,
North Yorkshire LA2 8HH

Tel: 015242 51203
Fax: 015242 51496

13 bedrooms, all with private bathroom; Free House; Historic interest; Bar and restaurant meals; Kendal 21 miles, Skipton 21.

Keith and Barbara Mannion invite you to their friendly eighteenth century residential coaching inn in the picturesque Dales village of Clapham. Ideal centre for walking the three peaks of Ingleborough, Pen-y-ghent and Whernside. All rooms have full en suite facilities, colour television and tea/coffee facilities. Enjoy good wholesome Yorkshire food in our restaurant, or bar meals in either of our two bars. Dogs welcome. Ring Barbara for details of special mid-week breaks. *ETB* ☜ ☜ ☜ *Commended.*

FALCON INN,
Whitby Road, Cloughton, Near Scarborough,
North Yorkshire YO13 0DY

Tel: 01723 870717

8 bedrooms, all with private bathroom; Free House with real ale; Bar and restaurant meals; Car park; Scarborough 4 miles; ££.

Standing in its own 7 acres of pasture and woodland with its southerly aspect towards the sea, this former coaching inn has recently been refurbished. The old coach house has been converted into the Carvery leaving the original inside stonework and most of the beams exposed. A wide selection of home-cooked English fare is served either here or in the bar lounge. This is a fine touring centre with several coastal resorts within easy reach. To the rear of the inn, a number of delightful bedrooms are furnished to a very high standard with full central heating, colour television and facilities for making hot drinks. *Les Routiers.*

THE STAR INN,
North Dalton, Near Driffield,
North Yorkshire YO25 9UX

Tel: 01377 217688

7 bedrooms, all with private bathroom; Free House with real ale; Historic interest; Bar and restaurant meals; Car park; Great Driffield 6 miles; ££.

Once a staging post on the Minster Way between York and Beverley, the Star Inn now offers the very best in Yorkshire hospitality to locals and visitors alike. Peacefully situated beside the pond, it is very much a village pub, offering traditional cask-conditioned ales and a selection of favourites such as fish, pies, lasagne, steaks, salads and sandwiches. Those fortunate individuals for whom time is not at a premium can relax in the Victorian Parlour à la carte restaurant, which features the finest food and wines, enhanced by courteous and efficient service and elegant surroundings. Of an equally high standard are the light and airy bedrooms, some of which overlook the pond. Set in the heart of the Yorkshire Wolds, this is a convenient base for exploring the many local attractions. ☜ ☜ ☜ ☜, *Egon Ronay.*

THE BLUE LION,
East Witton, Near Leyburn,   Tel: 01969 24273 (624273 from March '95)
North Yorkshire DL8 4SN   Fax: 01969 24189 (624189 from March '95)

9 bedrooms, all with private bathroom; Free House with real ale; Bar food, restaurant evenings only; Car park (30); Leyburn 4 miles, Middleham 2; ££££.

In the midst of an area of heather moorlands, waterfalls, limestone scars and remote valleys, the Blue Lion was built as a coaching inn in the 19th century. Recently refurbished, it still retains its period charm. It stands at the gateway to Wensleydale and Coverdale and is an ideal base for walking and touring excursions. The bar, with its open fire and flagstoned floor is warm and welcoming; hand-pulled traditional beers and an extensive range of bar meals may be enjoyed. The 40-cover candlelit restaurant provides a gracious setting for dinner with a choice of à la carte or table d'hôte menus. Bedrooms are furnished to a high standard and have bathrooms en suite, colour television and tea and coffee-making facilities.

ROYAL OAK HOTEL,
Great Ayton,   Tel: 01642 722361
North Yorkshire TS9 6BW   Fax: 01642 724047

5 bedrooms, all with private bathroom; Real ale; Historic interest; Children welcome; Bar and restaurant meals; Thirsk 23 miles, Middlesbrough 9.

The extensive dinner menu at the Royal Oak is not one for the indecisive. Ditherers will find themselves at closing time still unable to choose from delicious fillet dijon with its mustard and cream sauce, or perhaps pan-fried pork fillet with hot green peppers and cream. I would recommend speeding up the procedure by the tossing of coins — for whatever one selects one may be sure of the deepest satisfaction. Food is also available in the tastefully decorated, comfortably rustic bars, and guest bedrooms provide well appointed overnight accommodation, all having central heating, colour television and tea-making facilities.

TENNANT ARMS,
Kilnsey, Near Grassington,
North Yorkshire BD23 5PS
Tel: 01756 752301

10 bedrooms, all with private bathroom; Free House with real ale; Historic interest; Children welcome; Bar and restaurant meals; Grassington 3 miles; ££.

Friendly 17th century country inn hotel nestling under the famous Kilnsey Crag in the heart of Wharfedale, between the picturesque villages of Grassington and Kettlewell. The inn is run by the Douglas family who offer warm Yorkshire hospitality. All ten bedrooms are en suite. The cosy bars with log fires and beams serve delicious, individually prepared bar meals and hand-pulled ales; or dine in our beautiful pine-panelled dining room and choose from our extensive à la carte menu. Ideal for exploring the Dales. 👑 👑 👑 *Commended.*

MOUNT HOTEL,
Yorkersgate, Malton,
North Yorkshire YO17 0AB
Tel and Fax: 01653 692608

12 bedrooms, 5 with private bathroom; Free House with real ale; Historic interest; Bar and restaurant meals; Car park; York 17 miles; £/££.

With a number of well-known training stables in the area, horse racing enthusiasts have come to know this comfortable hotel well in company with tourists intent on exploring the North York Moors. The traditional bar has a welcoming open log fire whilst the delightful restaurant has an interesting minstrels' gallery and private bar. The à la carte and table d'hôte menus command attention and a vegetarian selection is available. Outside, the spacious car park is enclosed by private gardens where one may drink or dine 'al fresco' in warmer weather. Single, twin, double and family guest rooms provide a high standard of overnight accommodation, several with en suite facilities. 👑 👑, *Les Routiers.*

THE GREEN MAN,
15 Market Street, Malton,
North Yorkshire YO17 0LY
Tel: 01653 600370
Fax: 01653 696006

24 bedrooms, all with private bathroom; Free House with real ale; Historic interest; Bar and restaurant meals; Car park (50); York 17 miles; ££££.

For centuries, this elegant old coaching inn in the heart of a vibrant Yorkshire town regularly played host to the local gentry and now, following comprehensive refurbishment by English Rose Hotels in 1993, its fame has spread beyond those who held the secret. Its original features have been retained, even enhanced, and there can be few more enchanting places in which to drink than the beautifully panelled Oak Bars where first-rate bar snacks are also served. However, it is recommended that, if possible, appetites should be held in check in order to do full justice to an unforgettable meal in the Lot 15 Restaurant, so named because of the preponderance of auction houses in the town. Malton in delightful Ryedale is, of course, famous as a racehorse training centre and strings of thoroughbreds may regularly be seen exercising on the banks of the River Derwent. All the multifarious sporting, historic and scenic delights of North Yorkshire may be reached with ease from this splendid hotel and the fully en suite guest rooms ensure a comfortable and exquisitely decorated base from which to operate. The lovely Howard Suite does sterling service for receptions and other social functions and there are also excellent facilities for business meetings. Easy to find and easy to reach, the hotel has private parking for all guests. 👑 👑 👑 👑, *AA and RAC***, Johansens.*

THE YORKE ARMS,
Ramsgill-in-Nidderdale,
North Yorkshire HG3 5RL

Tel and Fax: 01423 755243

13 bedrooms, all with private bathroom; Free House; Historic interest; Bar food, restaurant evenings only, plus Sunday lunch; Car park (30); Pately Bridge 4 miles; ££££.

A lovely old creeper-clad inn in the heart of the Dales, where fine walks in the bracing moorland air will soon sweep away city tensions, and there are good opportunities for bird-watching, fishing, shooting and visiting local places of interest such as Studley Hall and Fountains Abbey. The Yorke Arms is just the place for a peaceful country holiday and offers warm and friendly hospitality within its substantial stone walls, where log fires, comfortable armchairs and gleaming brass gladden the eye and warm the heart. Excellent Yorkshire fare ranging from light meals and snacks in the bar to full restaurant meals will satisfy the heartiest appetite. *ETB* 🌷🌷🌷🌷 *Highly Commended, AA** and Red Rosette.*

THE BUCK INN,
Thornton Watlass, Near Bedale, Ripon,
North Yorkshire HG4 4AH

Tel: 01677 422461

5 bedrooms, all with private facilities; Free House with real ale; Children welcome; Bar food and dining area; Car park (25); Ripon 11 miles, Northallerton 9; ££.

Friendly country inn overlooking the delightful cricket green in a peaceful village just five minutes away from the A1. Newly refurbished bedrooms, all with en suite facilities, ensure that a stay at the Buck is both comfortable and relaxing. Delicious freshly cooked bar meals are served lunchtimes and evenings in the cosy bar and dining area. On Sundays a traditional roast with Yorkshire pudding is on the menu. Excellent Theakston, John Smiths, Black Sheep and Tetley cask beer is available, as is a regular guest ale. This is an ideal centre for exploring Herriot country. There is a children's playground in the secluded beer garden where quoits are also played. Midweek walking holidays organised throughout the year. 🌷🌷🌷 *Commended, AA*, CAMRA Good Pub Food Guide, Egon Ronay, Beer, Bed and Breakfast.*

NORTH YORKSHIRE – RICH IN TOURIST ATTRACTIONS!

Dales, moors, castles, abbeys, cathedrals – you name it and you're almost sure to find it in North Yorkshire. Leading attractions include Castle Howard, the moorlands walks at Goathland, the Waterfalls at Falling Foss, Skipton, Richmond, Wensleydale, Bridestones Moor, Ripon Cathedral, Whitby, Settle and, of course, York itself.

WHITE LION INN,
Cray, Buckden, Near Skipton,
North Yorkshire BD23 5JB
Tel: 01756 760262

5 bedrooms, all with private shower; Free House with real ale; Historic interest; Children welcome; Bar and restaurant meals; Car park; Hawes 9 miles.

Nestling beneath Buckden Pike at the head of Wharfedale, the White Lion Inn has been tastefully restored to offer five en suite bedrooms, while retaining its original beams, open log fires and stone-flagged floors. Traditional English fare is served in the bar or cosy dining room; children's menu available. The Inn provides a good choice of beers and spirits, including traditional hand-pulled ales, which in fine weather can be enjoyed in the beer garden. Parents can relax while children enjoy themselves in safety in the enclosed play area. The Inn is on the path of many recognised walks in the very heart of the Yorkshire Dales and makes an ideal base for touring and walking. The thriving market town of Skipton and Aysgarth with its famous falls are both less than half an hour away. There are also many sporting activities locally, including pony trekking, rock climbing, pot holing and golf. Pets welcome if well-behaved. Open all year. *CAMRA Pub of the Season 1991 for District.*

South Yorkshire

THE GRIFF INN,
Drakeholes, Near Bawtry, Doncaster,
South Yorkshire DN10 5DF
Tel: 01777 817206

3 bedrooms, all with private bathroom; Free House with real ale; Historic interest; Bar and restaurant meals; Car park (90); Doncaster 8 miles; £££.

Built over 200 years ago to serve the increased trade brought about by the building of the Chesterfield Canal, the inn also operated as a staging post for the mail coaches en route from Sheffield to Louth. With the arrival of the railway system, the canal began a long decline and even the coast road which once ran alongside the inn was diverted a few hundred yards away. Now largely restored, the canal has rekindled local life. In 1982, the inn was renovated and, in the hands of the Edmanson family, now aspires to hotel standards, particularly through the first-rate food served in its Drakes Carvery and Peach Restaurant and superb, spacious en suite accommodation.

West Yorkshire

HAREWOOD ARMS HOTEL,
Harrogate Road, Harewood, Near Leeds,
West Yorkshire LS17 9LH

Tel: 0113 2886566
Fax: 0113 2886064

24 bedrooms, all with private bathroom; Samuel Smith House; Bar and restaurant meals; Car park (60); Leeds 7 miles.

Solid and sturdy without, gracious and appealing within, this welcoming hostelry boasts an enviable reputation for both fine home-cooked fare and comfortable overnight accommodation in luxuriously appointed bedrooms overlooking gardens and terrace and the rolling hills beyond. All guest rooms are graced with private bath or shower, have tea and coffee facilities and colour television, and are furnished with as much care and concern as the public rooms. Snacks and hot and cold meals are cheerfully served lunchtime and evening in the bar which remains open all day, and the elegant surroundings of the restaurant are a fitting tribute to the à la carte cuisine on offer there. ♕ ♕ ♕ ♕, *RAC Comfort Merit Award.*

THE DUKE OF YORK INN,
West Street, Shelf, Halifax,
West Yorkshire HX3 7LN

Tel: 01422 202056
Fax: 01422 206618

12 bedrooms, all with private bathroom; Whitbread House with real ale; Historic interest; Bar and restaurant meals; Car park (30); Bradford 4 miles; ££.

If you are planning to walk the Calderdale Way or visit the unspoiled moors and dales, then make a note of this 17th century former coaching inn, which is the perfect place to stop for rest and refreshment. An above average choice of real ales, plus a comprehensive selection of beers, wines and spirits guarantees that thirsts will be fully quenched, while a glance at the menu is sure to bring a gleam to the eye of the hungry traveller. From sandwiches to steaks, all appetites are catered for, including an intriguing selection of home-made Indian dishes which will delight more exotic palates. Twelve neat bedrooms offer en suite bathrooms and colour television should overnight accommodation be required. *Les Routiers, Egon Ronay, CAMRA.*

The **£** symbol when appearing at the end of the italic section of an entry shows the anticipated price, during 1995, for **single full Bed and Breakfast.**

Under £30	£	**Over £45 but under £60**	£££
Over £30 but under £45	££	**Over £60**	££££

This is meant as an indication only and does not show prices for Special Breaks, Weekends, etc. Guests are therefore advised to verify all prices on enquiring or booking.

Recommended
WAYSIDE INNS
WALES

Clwyd

WHEATSHEAF INN,
Betws-yn-Rhos, Abergele,
Clwyd LL22 8AW

Tel: 01492 680218

4 bedrooms, all with private bathroom; Free House with real ale; Historic interest; Children welcome; Bar and restaurant meals; Car park (30); Abergele 4 miles; £.

An ale house in the 13th century and licensed as a coaching inn in the 17th century, this fascinating hostelry retains several attractive features including brass-strewn oak beams, stone pillars and original hayloft ladder. The warm atmosphere of the olde-worlde lounge bar is well in keeping with the mood, and dining by candlelight in the intimate restaurant is a rewarding experience. Beautifully placed in a picturesque village a little way inland from the main North Wales coastal resorts, the inn has a vibrant air about it with many events organised to attract young and not-so-young alike, cabaret and gourmet evenings and barbecues amongst them. Food, formal and casual, is excellent. 🏵️🏵️🏵️ *Commended.*

THE HAND HOTEL,
Llanarmon D.C, Near Llangollen,
Clywd LL20 7LD

Tel: 0169-176 666
Fax: 0169-176 262

14 bedrooms, all with private bathroom; Free House; Historic interest; Children welcome; Bar meals, restaurant evenings only; Car park (30); Llangollen 17 miles; ££/£££.

Our Hotel of 16th century origin nestles below mountains in a beautiful and tranquil village. We are nearest to the head of the Ceiriog Valley and provide a staging post on a truly scenic through-route to North and Mid Wales. The Hotel is also ideal for walking, pony-trekking, fishing or relaxing in comfortable old-world surroundings. National Trust properties within easy travelling distance include Erdvig, Chirk and Powis Castles. Snowdonia, Caernarfon, Portmeirion and Bodnant Gardens are reached easily. We have thirteen en suite bedrooms, each with television, direct dial phone, radio, tea-making facilities. We have an excellent oak-beamed restaurant with good food and wines. Local produce is used extensively. Log fires enhance the bar area as needed. The owner Lilian Brunton will be delighted to supply details of special terms for week-end and mid-week breaks. 🏵️🏵️🏵️ *Highly Commended, Ashley Courtenay, Egon Ronay Recommended.*

THE HAWK AND BUCKLE INN,
Llannefydd, Near Denbigh, Tel: 01745 79249; Fax: 01745 79316
Clwyd LL16 5ED (from June 1995 Tel: 01745 540249; Fax: 01745 540316)

10 bedrooms, all with private bathroom; Free House; Historic interest; Bar lunches and restaurant meals; Car park (20); Colwyn Bay 7 miles; ££.

Every 20th century comfort is to be found at this welcoming seventeenth-century village inn. All the en suite guest rooms in the tasteful extensions are equipped with telephone, tea/coffee making facilities and television; trouser press and hairdryer are available. Furnishings are comfortable and pleasing to the eye. Local game, pork, lamb and freshly caught salmon and trout are imaginatively served in the Inn's popular restaurant, and varied and substantial bar snacks are offered at lunchtime from 1st May to September 30th and every Wednesday and weekends. Hosts Robert and Barbara Pearson will happily supply a wealth of information on the area. Visa and Access are accepted. *WTB* ✿ ✿ ✿ *Highly Commended, Egon Ronay, Ashley Courtenay.*

YE OLDE ANCHOR INN,
Rhos Street, Ruthin, Tel: 01824 702813
Clwyd LL15 1DY Fax: 01824 703050

10 bedrooms, all with private bathroom; Free House; Historic interest; Bar and restaurant meals; Car park (20); Wrexham 14 miles; ££.

Low ceilings and sturdy oak beams remind patrons that this solidly constructed establishment has a long history of serving the needs of travellers since its 18th century origins as a stopping place for drovers on the road between Holyhead and Shropshire. Rest and refreshment are still the goals of those who cross its threshold nowadays, and they will not be disappointed by the standards of hospitality set by the proprietor, Rod England. A varied selection of freshly prepared bar meals and a full à la carte menu cater for the needs of the inner man, with of course a comprehensive range of real ales, beers, wines and spirits. The tastefully refurbished bedrooms offer every modern convenience, and make an ideal base for exploring this historic town, and indeed all of North Wales. ✿ ✿ ✿ *Highly Commended, AA** and Rosette for Food.*

Dyfed

CASTLE HOTEL,
Castle Square, Haverfordwest, Tel: 01437 769322
Dyfed SA61 2AA Fax: 01437 762740

9 bedrooms, all with private bathroom; Free House with real ale; Children welcome; Bar and restaurant meals; Broad Haven 7 miles; ££.

For those seeking the multifarious delights of West Wales, Haverfordwest is the perfect location with its ready accessibility to two coasts with a variety of sandy beaches, probably the best known Coastal Path in Britain and the many gems that await discovery in the Pembrokeshire National Park. Fitting the bill as the ideal base from which to plan such excursions, the comfortable, Victorian Castle Hotel stands in the town square in the shadow of the castle. Here one may find excellent refreshment in the bars and à la carte restaurant and with overnight accommodation enhanced by the provision of colour television and direct-dial telephone. Special weekend rates offer very good value. ✿ ✿ ✿ ✿, *AA **, Les Routiers.*

RISING SUN INN,
St. David's Road, Pelcomb Bridge, Haverfordwest,
Dyfed SA62 6EA
Tel: 01437 765171

2 bedrooms; Free House with real ale; Bar and restaurant meals; Car park (40); Haverfordwest 2 miles; ££.

1984 saw the construction of the present Rising Sun on the site of a former coaching inn, and in the past decade it has become a very popular part of the local community and a haven for summer visitors, providing friendly hospitality to all. Under the careful guidance of the resident chef, food here is particularly good, offering daily specials and lunchtime snacks in addition to traditional favourites and a varied vegetarian selection. House wines are available by the glass, and there is a comprehensive array of other refreshments. Two neat en suite bedrooms provide bed and breakfast accommodation, and an adjacent caravan and camping field can be pre-booked by those who enjoy the freedom of self-catering. ♛ ♛

THE FARMERS ARMS,
Mathry, Haverfordwest,
Dyfed SA62 5HB
Tel: 01348 831284

No accommodation; Free House with real ale; Historic interest; Bar food; Fishguard 6 miles.

There can be few eating places which can guarantee the freshness of their fish dishes in the way that the Farmers Arms can — it has its own boat, and, weather and tides permitting, can ensure the absolute minimum delay between sea and table. Naturally enough, all sorts of fish feature prominently on the lunchtime menu, but other tastes are well catered for, with delicious home-made soups, home-boiled hams, and filled rolls served in generous portions. The highlight of the menu is a seafood platter served with a whole lobster. The inn's popularity with local fishermen and farmers ensures no shortage of lively chat — this is just the spot to find out what is going on in the area.

THE BLACK LION HOTEL,
New Quay,
Dyfed SA45 9PT
Tel: 01545 560209
Fax: 01545 560585

7 bedrooms, 6 with private bathroom; Free House with real ale; Historic interest; Children welcome; Bar food, restaurant evenings only; Car park (30); Aberystwyth 19 miles; ££.

There is much to see and do in this picturesque little port, famous for its associations with Dylan Thomas, and not least of its attractions is the sturdy, stone-built Black Lion which overlooks the old harbour and the bay. The well stocked bar caters for thirsts great and small, while all appetites (and pockets!) will find something to suit on the menus offered in the bar and, more formally, in the oak-panelled dining room. Outside, all is equally pleasing, with a children's play area and a petanque pitch, as well as tables and chairs for use in finer weather. Comfortable bedrooms, mostly en suite, provide for the needs of the weary traveller. *AA ***.

THE ROYAL OAK INN,
Rhandirmwyn, Llandovery,
Tel: 015506 201; Fax: 015506 332
Dyfed SA20 0NY (from June 1995 Tel: 01550 760201 and Fax: 01550 760332)

5 bedrooms, 3 with private bathroom; Free House with real ale; Bar and restaurant meals; Car park (25); Llandovery 6 miles.

"Free and Easy" can sometimes be synonymous with slapdash and badly run, but one need have no such fears at the Royal Oak. The proprietors here have managed to combine informality with efficiency, and friendliness with courteous good service. Spacious rooms offer comfort as well as attractive decor and most have colour television and private facilities. The very full menu presented in the restaurant caters for most tastes, and bar snacks are available together with a nice range of local beers. Dinner is from 6.00 until 10.00pm, and sleepyheads will be pleased to note that breakfast will be served right up till 9.30 in the morning. *WTB* 👑, *AA Listed, Les Routiers Approved.*

THE TALBOT HOTEL,
The Square, Tregaron,
Dyfed SY25 6JL
Tel: 01974 298208

14 bedrooms, 5 with private bathroom; Free House with real ale; Historic interest; Children welcome; Bar and restaurant meals; Car park (30); Lampeter 10 miles; ££.

Those wishing to brush up their Welsh will find hosts Sally, Graham and Shân more than willing to converse with them in their native tongue, but non-linguists can rest assured that their welcome here will be equally cordial. This ancient inn's stone walls and oak beams are a constant reminder of its historic past and provide a most pleasant setting for enjoyment of the good food and ales on offer. A charming restaurant and a function room cater in admirable style for more formal requirements. Accommodation is equally attractive, with en suite bedrooms available if required. This lovely area affords ample opportunity for following traditional country pursuits. *WTB* 👑 👑, *AA *.*

Please mention
Recommended WAYSIDE INNS
when seeking refreshment or
accommodation at a Hotel
mentioned in these pages

Gwent

THREE SALMONS HOTEL,
Bridge Street, Usk,
Gwent NP5 1BQ

Tel: 01291 672133
Fax: 01291 673979

21 bedrooms, all with private bathroom; Free House with real ale; Historic interest; Bar and restaurant meals; Car park (45); Abergavenny 11 miles, Pontypool 7; £££.

Antiques, pictures and curios decorate the bar of this former coaching inn which enjoys a central situation in the pleasant town of Usk, famed as a livestock market as well as for the world-renowned salmon fishing on the river which shares its name. Good bar lunches are served daily as an informal alternative to luncheon in the oak-panelled restaurant, which also provides an elegant setting for evening dinner. Guest bedrooms of varying sizes to suit all requirements are available in the hotel itself, and further accommodation is situated in the Stables Annexe. The majority of rooms boast private facilities, and all have radio, telephone, colour television and tea trays. *WTB* 🌷 🌷 🌷 🌷, *AA/RAC ***.

RECOMMENDED SHORT BREAK HOLIDAYS
IN BRITAIN

Introduced by John Carter, TV Holiday Expert and Journalist

Specifically designed to cater for the most rapidly growing sector of the holiday market in the UK. Illustrated details of hotels offering special 'Bargain Breaks' throughout the year.

Available from newsagents and bookshops for £3.60 or direct from the publishers for £4.20 including postage, UK only.

FHG PUBLICATIONS LTD
Abbey Mill Business Centre, Seedhill,
Paisley, Renfrewshire PA1 1TJ

Gwynedd

PENHELIG ARMS,
Aberdovey,
Gwynedd LL35 0NF

Tel: 01654 767215
Fax: 01654 767690

10 bedrooms, all with private bathroom; Free House with real ale; Historic interest; Bar and restaurant meals; Car park (12); Machynlleth 9 miles.

The Penhelig Arms enjoys a superb position looking directly across the Dyfi estuary, and in fine weather visitors can sit outside by the sea wall and enjoy a drink or a meal. All but one of the charmingly appointed bedrooms have wonderful views of the sea and mountains beyond, and amenities such as en suite bathrooms, colour television, radio, and direct-dial telephones ensure that a stay here is truly relaxing. The hotel's excellent reputation has been built upon the first-class food served in the restaurant and in the more informal atmosphere of the bar. The restaurant is noted also for its award-winning wine list. Set on the edge of Snowdonia National Park, Aberdovey is an ideal centre for exploring Mid-Wales. *WTB ☖ ☖ ☖ ☖ Highly Commended, AA Rosette, Taste of Wales, Ashley Courtenay, CAMRA Good Pub Food, "Welsh Rarebits"*

GEORGE III HOTEL,
Penmaenpool, Dolgellau, Meirionnydd,
Gwynedd LL40 1YD

Tel: 01341 422525
Fax: 01341 423565

12 bedrooms, all with private bathrooms; Free House with real ale; Historic interest; Bar food, restaurant evenings only, plus Sun. lunch; Car park (100); Dolgellau 2 miles; ££££.

Beautifully situated at the head of the Mawddach Estuary, this charmingly individual establishment was once two separate buildings, pub and ship chandlers, which were united over a century ago to form the George III Hotel. Overnight guests may choose between accommodation in the hotel itself or in the Lodge a short step away. All rooms have private bathrooms, colour television, tea and coffee tray, hairdryer, direct-dial telephone and trouser press. Bar meals are served every day in the Dresser and Cellar Bar, and Sunday lunch may be taken in the restaurant where an excellent à la carte menu is available each evening. Free fishing permits for guests; mountain bike hire. *☖ ☖ ☖ ☖ Highly Commended, AA**RAC, Egon Ronay, Ashley Courtenay and Johansens.*

CORBETT ARMS HOTEL,
Corbett Square, Tywyn,
Gwynedd LL36 9DG

Tel: 01654 710264
Fax: 01654 710359

42 bedrooms, all with private bath or shower; Free House with real ale; Historic interest; Bar and restaurant meals; Car park; Machynlleth 10 miles; £.

A traditional inn offering exceptional value, situated on the Mid-Wales coast at Tywyn, on the edge of Snowdonia National Park. Facilities include a real ale pub with superb bar food, a traditional restaurant, a car park, and an enclosed Victorian garden. All bedrooms have private bath or shower and WC, and are comfortably furnished and equipped with colour television, direct-dial telephone and beverage making facilitites for tea and coffee; several rooms offer four-poster beds. Terms are 27 US dollars (£18) per person in rooms with private facilities, or try our Ghost Room (No. 36) where it is reputed that Mrs Stephens is sometimes in residence — 36 US dollars (£24) per person. Please note — terms quoted only apply in reference to this publication, please mention at time of booking. *WTB* 🌸 🌸 🌸, *AA and RAC**.*

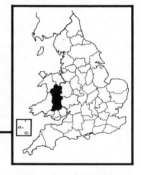

Powys

THE LION HOTEL & RESTAURANT,
Berriew, Near Welshpool,
Powys SY21 8PQ

Tel: 01686 640452/640844
Fax: 01686 640604

7 bedrooms, all with private bathroom; Free House with real ale; Historic interest; Bar food, restaurant evenings only; Car park (6); Welshpool 5 miles; £££/££££.

Prettier than any picture postcard, black and white timbered cottages cluster round the village church in this loveliest of spots on the Shropshire border. No less attractive is the Lion Hotel, which since the seventeenth century has provided friendly hospitality and good cheer to locals and visitors alike. Two cosy bars offer a good selection of real ales and other refreshments, with the added bonus of tasty, home-cookedmeals and snacks each day, supplemented in the evenings by an excellent and varied restaurant menu, where delicious Welsh specialities take their place beside English and Continental cuisine. Pretty, cottage-style en suite bedrooms provide all the comforts of home for those who find it impossible to tear themselves away. 🌸 🌸 🌸 🌸 *Highly Commended, AA**, Welsh Rarebits, Les Routiers, Johansens.*

THE GRIFFIN INN,
Llyswen, Brecon,
Powys LD3 0UR

Tel: 01874 754241
Fax: 01874 754592

8 bedrooms, 7 with private bathroom; Free House with real ale; Historic interest; Bar food, restaurant evenings only; Car park (12); Brecon 8 miles; ££.

A riot of colourful flowers in borders, tubs and hanging baskets give added charm to this creeper-clad inn during the summer months, and tables and chairs set outside enable one to enjoy them to the full. Inside, under the care of the Stockton family, everything is just as appealing and full of character. The heavily beamed bars are kept cosy by real fires when the weather is chilly, and guest bedrooms are spick and span, with comfortable furnishings. A wide range of good home-cooked dishes is available, and locally caught game, salmon and river trout feature well on the thoughtfully planned menus. There is a comfortable residents' lounge with separate television room. Pretty towns and villages have much to offer the tourist, good golfing is available, and the Griffin itself has fishing rights on the Upper Wye. *Commended, AA, Egon Ronay Pub of the Year 1989, B&B Pub of the Year 1992, Welsh Rarebits, Logis.*

UNICORN HOTEL,
Longbridge Street, Llanidloes,
Powys SY18 6EE

Tel and Fax: 01686 413167

5 bedrooms, all with private bathroom; Free House with real ale; Bar lunches, restaurant evenings only; Newtown 11 miles; ££.

Peaceful mid-Wales offers a variety of rural treasures awaiting discovery in its leafy valleys and rolling hills. The little town of Llanidloes, at the meeting of the Rivers Severn and Clywedog, is happily placed for such pleasurable exploration and one of the brightest jewels in its unassuming crown is this recently refurbished hotel where Proprietors, Derek and Chris Humphreys, extend a warm welcome to guests. Comfortable and friendly, the hotel offers superlative home cooking, a range of real and traditional ales and accommodation that would do credit to many a grander establishment. Beautifully furnished rooms, all en suite, are equipped with colour television and tea and coffee-making facilities and Bed and Breakfast terms are reasonable indeed. *Les Routiers.*

CASTLE INN,
Pengenffordd, Near Talgarth,
Powys LD3 0EP

Tel: 01874 711353

5 bedrooms, 2 with private bathroom; Free House with real ale; Children welcome; Bar food; Talgarth 4 miles; £.

The name "Castle Inn" derives from the ancient fortress of Castle Dinas which was at one time both Iron Age fort and Norman castle. It lies a short walk behind the Inn, which is situated in the rural heart of the Black Mountains in the Brecon Beacons National Park. This is an area very popular with those who love the great outdoors, with many activities available. The Inn offers accommodation in prettily decorated bedrooms, all with colour television and washbasins. In the evenings guests can relax by the log fire, perhaps with a choice from the economically priced menu of home-cooked dishes or from the selection of real ales. ♛♛ *Commended, AA QQ.*

Key to
Tourist Board Ratings

The Crown Scheme
(England, Scotland & Wales)

Covering hotels, motels, private hotels, guesthouses, inns, bed & breakfast, farmhouses. Every Crown classified place to stay is inspected annually. *The classification:* Listed then 1-5 Crown indicates the range of facilities and services. Higher quality standards are indicated by the terms APPROVED, COMMENDED, HIGHLY COMMENDED and DELUXE.

The Key Scheme
(also operates in Scotland using a Crown symbol)

Covering self-catering in cottages, bungalows, flats, houseboats, houses, chalets, etc. Every Key classified holiday home is inspected annually. *The classification:* 1-5 Key indicates the range of facilities and equipment. Higher quality standards are indicated by the terms APPROVED, COMMENDED, HIGHLY COMMENDED and DELUXE.

The Q Scheme
(England, Scotland & Wales)

Covering holiday, caravan, chalet and camping parks. Every Q rated park is inspected annually for its quality standards. The more √ in the Q – up to 5 – the higher the standard of what is provided.

Recommended
WAYSIDE INNS
SCOTLAND

Aberdeenshire

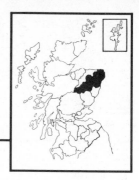

GORDON ARMS HOTEL,
Kincardine O'Neil,
Aberdeenshire AB34 5AA

Tel: 0133-98 84236

7 bedrooms, 5 with private bathroom; Free House with real ale; Historic interest; Children welcome; Bar and restaurant meals; Car park; Banchory 7 miles; £/££.

Early Victorian in origin when it was a coaching inn, the Gordon Arms is situated amidst the beautiful scenery of Royal Deeside where castles abound, including Balmoral, only half-an-hour away. The superb cuisine here is widely acknowledged, chef-inspired home-cooked dishes featuring locally caught salmon as well as succulent steaks and tempting sweets. Vegetarians are also well catered for. An interesting selection of organic wines is kept and also a fine range of real ales. Active outdoor pursuits abound in the area, including tennis, golf, fishing, pony trekking, water-skiing and even gliding. For such enthusiasts, comfortable accommodation in period style may be arranged. 🌸 🌸 🌸 *Approved.*

FOR THE MUTUAL GUIDANCE
OF GUEST AND HOST

Every year literally thousands of holidays, short-breaks and overnight stops are arranged through our guides, the vast majority without any problems at all. In a handful of cases, however, difficulties do arise about bookings, which often could have been prevented from the outset.

It is important to remember that when accommodation has been booked, both parties — guests and hosts — have entered into a form of contract. We hope that the following points will provide helpful guidance.

GUESTS: When enquiring about accommodation, be as precise as possible. Give exact dates, numbers in your party and the ages of any children. State the number and type of rooms wanted and also what catering you require — bed and breakfast, full board, etc. Make sure that the position about evening meals is clear — and about pets, reductions for children or any other special points.

Read our reviews carefully to ensure that the proprietors you are going to contact can supply what you want. Ask for a letter confirming all arrangements, if possible.

If you have to cancel, do so as soon as possible. Proprietors do have the right to retain deposits and under certain circumstances to charge for cancelled holidays if adequate notice is not given and they cannot re-let the accommodation.

HOSTS: Give details about your facilities and about any special conditions. Explain your deposit system clearly and arrangements for cancellations, charges, etc, and whether or not your terms include VAT.

If for any reason you are unable to fulfil an agreed booking without adequate notice, you may be under an obligation to arrange alternative suitable accommodation or to make some form of compensation.

While every effort is made to ensure accuracy, we regret that FHG Publications cannot accept responsibility for errors, omissions or misrepresentation in our entries or any consequences thereof. Prices in particular should be checked because we go to press early. We will follow up complaints but cannot act as arbiters or agents for either party.

Argyll

CAIRNDOW STAGECOACH INN,
Cairndow,
Argyll PA26 8BN

Tel: 01499 600286
Fax: 01499 600220

12 bedrooms, 10 with shower and toilet; Free House with real ale; Historic interest; Children welcome; Bar and restaurant meals; Car park (35); Arrochar 12 miles, Inveraray 10.

Amidst the beautiful scenery which characterises the upper reaches of Loch Fyne, this historic stagecoach inn enjoys a spectacular sheltered position. In the delightful restaurant one may dine well by candlelight from the table d'hôte and à la carte menus; bar meals are served all day. There is also a new functions bar and games room. Bedrooms are centrally heated, with radio, television, direct-dial telephone, baby listening, and tea making facilities. There are two de-luxe rooms with two-person spa baths, king-size beds and 20" television! This is an ideal spot for touring Oban, the Western Highlands, Glencoe, the Trossachs, the Cowal Peninsula, Kintyre and Campbeltown. The inn is under the personal supervision of hosts Mr and Mrs Douglas Fraser, and the area offers fine opportunities for many outdoor pursuits and visits. Lochside beer garden, exercise room, sauna and solarium.

WHISTLEFIELD INN,
Loch Eck, By Dunoon,
Argyll PA23 8SQ

Tel: 0136986 440

6 bedrooms; Free House; Historic interest; Children welcome; Bar and restaurant meals; Car park; Dunoon 10 miles; £.

Built in 1663, this fine old drovers' inn has been dispensing good hospitality and a cheerful welcome to many a footsore traveller over the years, and now greets tourists and visitors from all over the world who come to discover this peaceful, uncommercialised part of Scotland. Naturally fishing is a popular local activity, and permits for salmon fishing may be bought at the hotel and boats hired to explore the loch. The comfortable accommodation includes two bedrooms which open onto a small patio area and enjoy breathtaking views of mountains and loch. A tasty range of bar meals and snacks is available.

LOCHNELL ARMS HOTEL,
North Connel,
Argyll PA37 1RP
Tel: 01631 71408

11 bedrooms, 7 with private bathroom; Tennent Caledonian House; Historic interest; Children welcome; Bar food; Car park (20); Oban 5 miles.

Coming from the south, one's first view of this solid whitewashed hotel is across the sparkling waters of Loch Etive just before Connel Bridge, and so appealing is the picture it makes, one's spirits are immediately lifted. A family concern, the warmth of the welcome at the Lochnell is as much part of its charm as the magnificent view, clean and comfortable guest rooms (most with private facilities), and varied and interesting cuisine. Meals and snacks can be taken both lunchtime and evening in the lounge bar with conservatory, and the extensive menu features homemade chilli, fish and steaks. Well kept gardens roll down to the beach. Children are warmly welcomed, as indeed are the over fifty-fives who are subject to special discounts for a three-day midweek stay excepting July and August. Nearby attractions include the busy and picturesque town of Oban, Sea Life Centre, Rare Breeds Park and a host of cruising opportunities.

INSHAIG PARK HOTEL,
Easdale, Seil Island, By Oban,
Argyll PA34 4RF
Tel: 01852 300256

6 bedrooms, all with private bathroom; Free House; Bar and restaurant meals; Car park; Oban 16 miles; ££.

The famous eighteenth century "Bridge over the Atlantic" takes one onto Seil Island and Easdale where you will find this comfortable Victorian hotel, set in its own grounds overlooking the sea and the scattered islands of the Inner Hebrides. This family-run hotel has six comfortable bedrooms, all with central heating, colour television, and tea-making facilities. Meals can be taken either in the bar (over 40 malt whiskies to sample) or in the dining room overlooking the sea. Fresh local seafood is a speciality. An ideal place for an "away from it all" holiday. 🌷🌷🌷 *Commended, Les Routiers.*

Available from most bookshops, the 1995 edition of THE GOLF GUIDE covers details of every UK golf course – well over 2000 entries – for holiday or business golf. Hundreds of hotel entries offer convenient accommodation, accompanying details of the courses – the 'pro', par score, length etc.

Endorsed by The Professional Golfers' Association (PGA) and including Holiday Golf in Ireland, France, Portugal, Spain and the USA.

£8.50 from bookshops or £9.50 including postage (UK only) from FHG Publications, Abbey Mill Business Centre, Paisley PA1 1TJ.

THE BARN BAR COUNTRY INN,
Lerags, By Oban,   Tel: 01631 64501; Fax: 01631 66925
Argyll PA34 4SE   (changing to Tel: 01631 564501/Fax: 01631 566925)

Accommodation in self catering chalets; Children welcome; Bar and restaurant meals; Car park; Oban 3 miles.

This friendly country inn is situated on Cologin Farm, which offers accommodation in warm, well insulated, fully equipped timber bungalows (STB Three/Four Crowns Commended). The Barn serves outstanding home-made meals throughout the day, and in the evenings there is a range of Scottish entertainment. Oban is just three miles away, and from there ferries sail to the Western Isles; other activities available locally include hill walking, water sports, birdwatching, tennis, golf etc. On site amenities include a games room, shop and launderette. Farm pets include ducks, hens, guinea pigs and rabbits; own pets welcome at no extra cost. Open all year round. Colour brochure available on request.

Ayrshire

THE FENWICK HOTEL,
A77 Ayr Road, Fenwick, By Kilmarnock,   Tel: 01560 600478
Ayrshire KA3 6AU   Fax: 01560 600731

12 bedrooms, 9 with private bathroom; Free House with real ale; Children welcome; Bar and restaurant meals; Car park (150); Kilmarnock 4 miles; £££.

Standing at the side of the main road between Ayr and Glasgow, and convenient also for the coast and the many local golf courses (20 within 20 miles!), the welcoming Fenwick Hotel offers traditional Scottish hospitality at its finest. Stop off for a meal or refreshment and you will find a comprehensive menu offering a wide range of dishes, from traditional fish, chicken and steaks to more exotic fare such as Cajun Chicken and Prawn and Smoked Salmon Crepes; a selection of sandwiches, salads, etc caters for lighter appetites. If you are fortunate enough to be able to stay for a night or two (or longer), fully refurbished en suite bedrooms boast a full range of amenities, including king-size beds, colour television, and hairdryers. ♥ ♥ ♥ Commended, Taste of Scotland.

Dumfriesshire

BALMORAL HOTEL,
High Street, Moffat,
Dumfriesshire DG10 9DL

Tel: 01683 20288
Fax: 01683 20451

16 bedrooms, 6 with private bathroom; Free House with real ale; Historic interest; Children welcome; Bar and restaurant meals; Car park; Dumfries 19 miles; ££.

Once the centre of the Scottish woollen trade and a popular spa, Moffat nestles in the gentle Annandale valley, providing both a good centre for touring the Border country and a rather pleasing holiday venue in itself, with good golfing, fishing, shooting, hill-walking and pony trekking. Accommodation in this substantial old inn run by John and Pip Graham comprises sixteen comfortable and well furnished bedrooms, some en suite and all with tea and coffee facilities and colour television. A character-filled lounge bar, dining room and residents' lounge complete the guest accommodation, and fine Scottish fare is served with charm and quiet courtesy.

THE RED HOUSE HOTEL,
Newton Wamphray, Near Moffat,
Dumfriesshire DG10 9NF

Tel: 01576 470470

4 bedrooms, 2 with private bathroom; Free House; Bar meals, restaurant evenings only; Car park (12); Moffat 6 miles; ££.

Enjoy comfortable farmhouse style bed and breakfast and personal attention at the Red House. It is situated just 600 yards from the River Annan and enjoys spectacular views of the Moffat Hills. Sporting salmon and trout fishing is available, and guests can enjoy excellent walking and birdwatching within a few minutes' drive in the Wamphray Glen. Horse riding, golf courses and craft centres are within easy reach.

The **£** symbol when appearing at the end of the italic section of an entry shows the anticipated price, during 1995, for **single full Bed and Breakfast.**

Under £30	£	**Over £45 but under £60** £££
Over £30 but under £45 ££		**Over £60** ££££

This is meant as an indication only and does not show prices for Special Breaks, Weekends, etc. Guests are therefore advised to verify all prices on enquiring or booking.

Edinburgh & Lothians

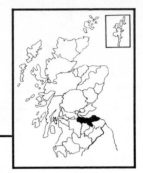

BLACKNESS INN,
18 The Square, Blackness, Linlithgow,
West Lothian EH49 7JA

Tel: 01506 834252

5 bedrooms with private facilities; Free House with real ale; Children welcome; Bar and restaurant meals, lunchtime and evenings; Car park; Bo'ness 4 miles; £.

The village of Blackness, with its 14th century castle built in the shape of a ship, was once a very busy seaport, but is now a quiet backwater, bypassed by the hurly burly of modern life. The castle was the setting for Zefferelli's "Hamlet". This two-storey white-washed inn offers the visitor a choice of either a quiet drink in the public bar or an excellent meal in the lounge bar, where oak tables and red upholstered chairs add lots of character. In the winter months open fires in both bars maake the inn even more welcoming. There are four comfortable bedroom and a residents' lounge; food is available each day until 10pm. Situated on the foreshore, off the main Queensferry to Linlithgow road, this is a very pleasant "local", with good facilities and a lively atmosphere. *STB Approved. Winner Seafood Authority Awards. Good Beer Guide.*

Key to
Tourist Board Ratings

The Crown Scheme
(England, Scotland & Wales)

Covering hotels, motels, private hotels, guesthouses, inns, bed & breakfast, farmhouses. Every Crown classified place to stay is inspected annually. *The classification:* Listed then 1-5 Crown indicates the range of facilities and services. Higher quality standards are indicated by the terms APPROVED, COMMENDED, HIGHLY COMMENDED and DELUXE.

The Key Scheme
(also operates in Scotland using a Crown symbol)

Covering self-catering in cottages, bungalows, flats, houseboats, houses, chalets, etc. Every Key classified holiday home is inspected annually. *The classification:* 1-5 Key indicates the range of facilities and equipment. Higher quality standards are indicated by the terms APPROVED, COMMENDED, HIGHLY COMMENDED and DELUXE.

The Q Scheme
(England, Scotland & Wales)

Covering holiday, caravan, chalet and camping parks. Every Q rated park is inspected annually for its quality standards. The more √ in the Q – up to 5 – the higher the standard of what is provided.

Fife

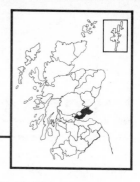

ABERDOUR HOTEL,
38 High Street, Aberdour,
Fife KY3 0SW

Tel: 01383 860325
Fax: 01383 860808

11 bedrooms, all with private bathroom; Free House with real ale; Historic interest; Bar meals, restaurant evenings only; Car park (8); Burntisland 3 miles; £££.

Specialising in traditional cooking and real ales, the Aberdour Hotel offers guests a warm Scottish welcome in one of Fife's picturesque coastal villages. Although dating back to the 17th century, the hotel has recently been upgraded to provide all modern facilities. However, links with the past remain; the courtyard stables at the rear date from 1648 and the cellar is reputed to be 400 years old. The restaurant is full of character with its beamed ceilings and stone and wood panelled walls. Excellent home-cooked meals are served here and also in the lounge bar with its open coal fire. Guest rooms now have en suite facilities, colour television and tea and coffee-makers. *STB* 🌷 🌷 🌷 *Commended, AA QQQ Commended.*

MELDRUMS HOTEL,
Ceres, Near Cupar,
Fife KY15 5NW

Tel: 01334 828286
Fax: 01334 828795

7 bedrooms, all with private bathroom; Free House with real ale; Historic interest; Bar and restaurant meals; Car park (15); Cupar 3 miles; £££.

Virtually a golfer's paradise, this comfortable hotel is situated in the picturesque village of Ceres, just six miles from the home of golf — St. Andrews and, unbelievably, within easy driving (!) distance of no less than 56 other courses, many of them famous. By way of variety, the quaint fishing villages of the Kingdom of Fife lie close at hand. The hotel caters splendidly for family parties and the accommodation is of a high standard, all rooms being centrally heated and having en suite facilities, colour television, radio, hairdryer and tea and coffee-makers. Excellent meals are served in a cosy restaurant whilst, outside, there is a beer garden with swings for the children and a practice golf net. 🌷 🌷 🌷 *Commended.*

Please mention
Recommended WAYSIDE INNS
when seeking refreshment or
accommodation at a Hotel
mentioned in these pages

Inverness-shire

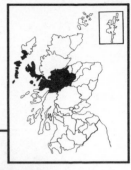

ARISAIG HOTEL,
Arisaig,
Inverness-shire PH39 4NH

Tel: 01687 450210
Fax: 01687 450310

15 bedrooms, 6 with private bathroom; Free House; Historic interest; Children welcome; Bar and restaurant meals; Car park (30); Fort William 37 miles, Mallaig 7; ££.

This historic Jacobite inn stands on the shores of Loch Nan Ceal with views across the bay to the isles of Skye, Muck, Rhum and Eigg. The proprietors, Malcolm and Jacqueline Ross, welcome you to their warm family atmosphere, where you can relax and enjoy the chance to explore this unspoiled area. All bedrooms have direct-dial telephone, remote-control colour television and tea/coffee making facilities; rooms with private bathrooms are available. Cuisine is based upon traditional and modern presentation of fresh produce from Scotland's natural larder, especially locally caught seafood, and can be enjoyed in the restaurant or, more informally, in the bar. An extensive wine list is available, as well as a superb range of malt whiskies. ♚ ♚ *Commended, AA and RAC **.*

HIGHLAND REGION — AND THE ISLANDS TOO!

From the genteel town of Inverness to the ragged formations of the west coast and on, over the sea to Skye and many more islands — yes Highland Region is vast! You'll probably not find that many people but places that most definitely should be found include the Caledonian Canal, Culloden, Mallaig, Loch Ness, Inverewe, Duncansby Head, Ben Nevis, the Cairngorms, Golspie, and the Islands themselves.

TOMICH HOTEL,
Tomich Holidays, By Beauly,
Inverness-shire IV4 7LY

Tel: 01456 415399

8 bedrooms, all with private bathroom; Children welcome; Car park; Inverness 30 miles.

Two miles south of Glen Affric, in a conservation area in the heart of the Highlands and tastefully refurbished to retain its Victorian charm, you will find the Tomich Hotel. Already famous as a fishing hotel, it offers the perfect location for walking, touring or just relaxing. It is only 30 miles from Inverness and within striking distance of Skye, Fort William, Ullapool and Loch Ness. From the formal comfort of the dining room to the oak-beamed cosiness of the bar, or from the hotel gardens and pond to the warmth of the indoor pool, you are assured of an enjoyable stay. Accommodation is also available in a family complex in hotel grounds outwith the hotel. A courtesy car can provide transport to and from the hotel to the airport or train station. *STB* 🌸 🌸 🌸 🌸 *Commended.*

NETHER LOCHABER HOTEL,
Onich, Fort William,
Inverness-shire PH33 6SE

Tel: 01855 821235

5 bedrooms; Free House; Historic interest; Bar and restaurant meals; Car park, garages (2); Edinburgh 121 miles, Glasgow 91, Oban 48, Fort William 10; ££.

An ideal centre from which to explore Lochaber, the Ardnamurchan Peninsula and Glencoe. This old Highland inn may be small, but it is a homely place which has been run by the MacKintosh family since 1923. Traditional home cooking goes hand in hand with homely service, comfortable accommodation and private facilities. The inn stands on the shores of beautiful Loch Linnhe at Corran Ferry.

The £ symbol when appearing at the end of the italic section of an entry shows the anticipated price, during 1995, for **single full Bed and Breakfast.**

Under £30	**£**	**Over £45 but under £60**	**£££**
Over £30 but under £45	**££**	**Over £60**	**££££**

This is meant as an indication only and does not show prices for Special Breaks, Weekends, etc. Guests are therefore advised to verify all prices on enquiring or booking.

Isle of Mull

CRAIGNURE INN,
Craignure,
Isle of Mull PA65 6AY

Tel: 016802 305

Fax: 016802 470

4 bedrooms; Free House; Historic interest; Bar food; Car park (20); Car ferry from Oban; £.

A listed building, this former drovers' inn is reputed to date back to 1695, but today's visitor may be assured of comforts vastly superior to those enjoyed by the cattlemen who rested here on their journey to the mainland. Personally supervised by the proprietor, the inn has four cosy guest rooms, all with tea-making facilities, heating, electric blankets and washbasins. Bar meals and packed lunches are available and the small intimate dining room boasts Scottish and European specialities. Mull is easily accessible by car ferry and holds as much for the sporting enthusiast as for those seeking the peace and quiet of an island retreat.

FOR THE MUTUAL GUIDANCE
OF GUEST AND HOST

Every year literally thousands of holidays, short-breaks and overnight stops are arranged through our guides, the vast majority without any problems at all. In a handful of cases, however, difficulties do arise about bookings, which often could have been prevented from the outset.

It is important to remember that when accommodation has been booked, both parties — guests and hosts — have entered into a form of contract. We hope that the following points will provide helpful guidance.

GUESTS: When enquiring about accommodation, be as precise as possible. Give exact dates, numbers in your party and the ages of any children. State the number and type of rooms wanted and also what catering you require — bed and breakfast, full board, etc. Make sure that the position about evening meals is clear — and about pets, reductions for children or any other special points.

Read our reviews carefully to ensure that the proprietors you are going to contact can supply what you want. Ask for a letter confirming all arrangements, if possible.

If you have to cancel, do so as soon as possible. Proprietors do have the right to retain deposits and under certain circumstances to charge for cancelled holidays if adequate notice is not given and they cannot re-let the accommodation.

HOSTS: Give details about your facilities and about any special conditions. Explain your deposit system clearly and arrangements for cancellations, charges, etc, and whether or not your terms include VAT.

If for any reason you are unable to fulfil an agreed booking without adequate notice, you may be under an obligation to arrange alternative suitable accommodation or to make some form of compensation.

While every effort is made to ensure accuracy, we regret that FHG Publications cannot accept responsibility for errors, omissions or misrepresentation in our entries or any consequences thereof. Prices in particular should be checked because we go to press early. We will follow up complaints but cannot act as arbiters or agents for either party.

Kinross-shire

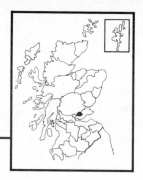

LOMOND COUNTRY INN, Kinnesswood, By Loch Leven, Kinross-shire KY13 7HN

Tel: 01592 840253
Fax: 01592 840693

12 bedrooms, all with private bathroom; Free House with real ale; Children welcome; Bar food, restaurant evenings only; Car park (50); Minathort 6 miles; ££.

On the slopes of the Lomond Hills, overlooking Loch Leven, the Lomond Country Inn is at the hub of all the sporting, cultural and leisure opportunities that abound across the broad band of central Scotland. Kinnesswood is ten minutes from the M90 which links Perth with Edinburgh. Within an hour's drive there are over 50 golf courses and facilities for fishing, shooting, riding, hill walking and bird watching, fine country houses to visit, plus the delights of the Fife coast; Edinburgh is 40 minutes away and Glasgow less than an hour. Providing a high standard of service, food and accommodation at sensible prices, the inn has pleasant public areas with open fires and a friendly, informal atmosphere. Bar meals are served at lunchtime and in the evening whilst the restaurant has interesting à la carte and fixed-priced menus comprising Scottish dishes and local specialities. Advantage is taken of fresh local produce, sea and freshwater fish, game, beef, lamb, vegetables and fruit in season. An excellent place in which to stay for a rewarding touring/sporting holiday, the inn has twelve guest rooms, all with en suite facilities; four of them are in the main building and eight in a recent extension adjacent. All rooms have colour television and direct-dial telephones. There is a swimming pool and leisure facilities in Kinross, a 9 hole golf course adjoining the inn and several delightful loch-side picnic spots nearby. ♣ ♣ ♣ *Commended, AA Rosette, Taste of Scotland, Logis of Great Britain.*

Peeblesshire

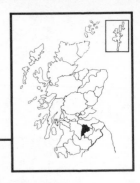

TRAQUAIR ARMS,
Traquair Road, Innerleithen,
Peeblesshire EH44 6PD

Tel: 01896 830229
Fax: 01896 830260

10 bedrooms, all with private bathroom; Free House with real ale; Children welcome; Bar and restaurant meals; Car park (25); Peebles 6 miles.

A solidly constructed traditional nineteenth-century Scottish inn, just 40 minutes from Edinburgh and 10 minutes from Peebles, in a delightful Borders valley. Hugh and Marian Anderson run it as a relaxing, friendly, family-run hotel with genuine concern for the comfort of their guests. Imaginative menus utilise the best local produce, and in appropriate weather can be enjoyed beside a blazing log fire in the dining room or al fresco in the secluded garden. The bar prides itself on its real ales. Egon Ronay's "Good Pub Guide" says: "Bed and breakfast is recommended, particularly the handsome Scottish meal complete with superb kippers". *STB* 👑 👑 👑 *Commended, Taste of Scotland, CAMRA, Best Breakfast in Britain 1990, "In Britain" Scottish Finalist 1993.*

NOTE

All the information in this book is given in good faith in the belief that it is correct. However, the publishers cannot guarantee the facts given in these pages, neither are they responsible for changes in policy, ownership or terms that may take place after the date of going to press. Readers should always satisfy themselves that the facilities they require are available and that the terms, if quoted, still apply.

KINGSMUIR HOTEL,
Springhill Road, Peebles,
Peeblesshire EH45 9EP

Tel: 01721 720151
Fax: 01721 721795

10 bedrooms, all with private bathroom; Free House with real ale; Bar and restaurant meals lunchtime and evenings; Car park (25); Edinburgh 20 miles; £££.

Peebles is a Royal and Ancient Burgh with many fine shops and easy access to the stately houses and castles of the Borders. The Kingsmuir is a century-old country house, set in leafy grounds looking across parkland to the River Tweed. It is a family-run hotel offering friendly, efficient service and comfortable surroundings, with the original character of the building still clearly evident. Many awards have been won for the traditional Scottish cooking. Vegetarians, children and those with smaller appetites are catered for separately, with restaurant menus selected daily and a wide choice from the bar lunch and supper menus. ♛♛♛ *Commended, Taste of Scotland, Les Routiers.*

Perthshire

THE LADE INN,
Kilmahog, By Callander,
Perthshire FK17 8HD

Tel: 01877 330152
Fax: 01877 331078

2 bedrooms, both with private bathroom; Free House with real ale; Children welcome; Bar and restaurant meals; Car park (30); Stirling 14 miles; ££.

If visiting the charming village of Callander and overcome by pangs of hunger, it is well worth driving on for just one more mile, for nestled in a secluded spot stands this friendly, stone-built inn. The proprietors and staff offer a warm welcome to the many visitors who are drawn to this most scenic area, and the inn has had glowing recommendations in many leading guides. Appetising lunchtime bar meals and a more extensive evening menu are served in generous helpings, with the emphasis on the freshest of local produce, and an equally impressive range of refreshments includes real ales and some good wines by the glass. Two spacious double/twin bedrooms provide comfortable overnight accommodation. ♛♛♛ *Commended.*

TORMAUKIN HOTEL,
Glendevon, By Dollar,
Perthshire FK14 7JY

Tel: 01259 781252

Fax: 01259 781526

10 bedrooms, all with private bathroom; Free House with real ale; Historic interest; Bar food, restaurant evenings only; Car park (50); Auchterarder 6 miles; ££££.

Built as a drovers' inn around the time of Bonnie Prince Charlie's birth, the Tormaukin Hotel has been offering rest and refreshment for over 270 years, and today that honourable tradition is maintained by host Marianne Worthy. Those wishing to dine informally in the bar will find a most acceptable lunch and supper menu which includes some excellent vegetarian dishes, and the à la carte restaurant is open nightly to provide fine fare and fine wines in the pleasantest of surroundings. Bedrooms are individually decorated and have colour television, private bathroom, tea and coffee facilities, direct-dial telephone and radio alarm. *STB* ❦ ❦ ❦ *Commended, Egon Ronay, Johansen, Good Pub Guide.*

LONGFORGAN COACHING INN,
Main Street, Longforgan, By Dundee,
Perthshire DD2 5EU

Tel: 01382 360386

20 bedrooms, all with private bathroom; Children welcome; Dundee 4 miles; ££.

The Coaching Inn has recently been refurbished to provide 20 twin/double bedrooms in the original 18th century inn and stable block. All bedrooms have en suite bathroom, colour television, direct-dial telephone, trouser press, ironing facilities, hairdryer and tea/coffee making. Adjacent to the A90 Perth-Dundee trunk route, ideal for fishing, shooting and golfing breaks (close to Carnoustie, St. Andrews, Gleneagles) and visiting Glamis, Perth, Dundee, etc. All rooms from £32.50 *per room.*

LITTER!
DON'T GO HOME
WITHOUT IT

TIDY BRITAIN GROUP

TIDY TRAVEL

Ross-shire

APPLECROSS HOTEL,
Applecross, Wester Ross,
Ross-shire IV54 8LR

Tel: 0152-04 262

5 bedrooms; Free House; Bar food, restaurant evenings only (booking required); Car park; Shieldaig 20 miles; £.

The very remoteness of the Applecross Peninsula is one of its attractions but, on a practical note, this fine hostelry commands immediate attention. With magnificent views overlooking the Inner Sound and the island of Raasay with the Cuillin Hills of Skye forming a dramatic backdrop, this is a naturalist's paradise beckoning, in particular, the hill-walker, angler and ornithologist, whilst the ski resort of Aviemore is just over an hour's drive away. The inn-cum-hotel specialises in an exciting variety of fresh, locally caught seafood as well as steaks and local venison. Bar meals are available all day. A note to would-be escapees — the Bed and Breakfast accommodation is reasonable in price but in great demand. *Egon Ronay, AA, Good Pub Guide.*

PLEASE ENCLOSE A STAMPED
ADDRESSED ENVELOPE WHEN
WRITING TO ENQUIRE ABOUT
ACCOMMODATION FEATURED IN
THIS GUIDE

ACHILTY HOTEL,
Contin,
Ross-shire IV14 9EG

Tel: 01997 421355
Fax: 01463 792780

12 bedrooms, all with private bathroom; Free House; Historic interest; Children welcome; Bar and restaurant meals; Car park (50); Strathpeffer 2 miles; £/££.

Ideally situated 20 minutes from Inverness on the Ullapool road, surrounded by spectacular scenery. The Achilty, a former Coaching Inn, combines the old world charm of log fires etc. with modern amenities, creating a real homely atmosphere. All bedrooms have private facilities. Excellent cuisine with choice of bar supper menu or à la carte restaurant, including vegetarian and children's menus. Open all year. Special rates for three nights and weekly stays. *Ross & Cromarty Tourist Board* 👑 👑 👑, *AA***.

THE OLD INN,
Gairloch,
Ross-shire IV21 2BD

Tel: 01445 2006
Fax: 01445 2445

14 bedrooms, all with private bathroom; Free House with real ale; Historic interest; Bar and restaurant meals; Car park (50); Inverness 71 miles, Ullapool 56.

Recently featured on TV's top holiday programme, "Wish You Were Here!". The famous gardens of Inverewe are just seven miles from this solid and welcoming family-run inn, and guests booking for three nights' dinner, bed and breakfast may visit them free of charge. Real ales are a speciality, and good bar food is served here daily. Both table d'hôte and à la carte menus are offered in the dining room, locally caught seafood, trout and salmon vying for the gourmet's attention with fine Aberdeen Angus beef and skilfully prepared venison. Colour television, beverage makers, direct-dial telephones and child/baby listening facilities are provided in each of the en suite guestrooms, all of which are furnished for comfort as well as being pleasing to the eye. *STB* 👑 👑 👑 *Commended, AA/RAC ***.

MILLCROFT HOTEL,
Gairloch,
Ross-shire IV21 2BT

Tel: 01445 712376
Fax: 01445 712091

Bedrooms all with private bathroom, self catering accommodation also available; Restaurant meals; Poolewe 6 miles.

Enjoy home comforts by the lochside with panoramic views of Skye and the Torridon mountains. Accommodation is available in comfortable en suite bedrooms, all with clock radio, hairdryer and beverage maker. There are also self-contained two-bedroom flats with colour television and sea views. The restaurant features fresh local seafood. Other amenities include lounge and public bars, a coin-operated laundry and mountain bike hire. Day or overnight trips can be arranged in our sailing cruisers for short local sails or to the the islands of the Inner Sound, ideal for novices, the more experienced or naturalists. Village amenities are one minute's walk away; sandy beaches, nine-hole golf course, Inverewe Garden, Heritage Museum and swimming pool are all close by. Ideal for a restful or active break.

Roxburghshire

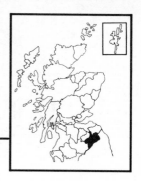

PLOUGH INN,
Lilliesleaf, Melrose,
Roxburghshire TD6 9JD

Tel: 01835 870271

3 bedrooms, all with private bathroom; Free House with real ale; Bar food, restaurant evenings only; Car park (20); Hawick 7 miles; ££.

Unpretentious but a really comfortable 'home from home', the Plough Inn is situated in a charming village as pretty as its name. For touring the historic Border towns, abbeys and stately homes, this is a fine place in which to stay or even call in for refreshment. Bedrooms are immaculate and there is a well-furnished sitting room for guests overlooking the garden. Terms for Bed and Breakfast are very reasonable. Under the Proprietorship of Douglas Hannah, a variety of good ales and spirits is on offer and the inn's worthy food menu includes some interesting dishes with a selection of delicious sweets always available. 🏵 🏵 🏵 Commended.

Selkirkshire

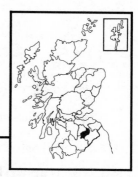

CLOVENFORDS HOTEL,
1 Vine Street, Clovenfords, Near Galashiels,
Selkirkshire TD1 3LU

Tel: 01896 850203
Fax: 01896 850596

4 bedrooms, all with private bathroom; Free House with real ale; Historic interest; Children welcome; Bar and restaurant meals; Car park; Galashiels 3 miles; ££.

A statue of Sir Walter Scott (a former guest) greets one at the door of this early eighteenth-century Tweed Valley hostelry which offers a solid and comfortable base for any Borders break. Accommodation is limited to just four guest rooms, two twin and two double, creating the intimate atmosphere of a house party, and all have either shower or bath en suite, television and tea/coffee making facilities. Morning coffee, good bar lunches and suppers, and that delightful Scottish institution of high tea are served with cheerful efficiency. All in all, an ideal base for exploring this most historic and scenic area. 🏵 🏵 🏵

Stirlingshire

THE EAGLETON HOTEL,
103 Henderson Street, Bridge of Allan,
Stirlingshire FK9 4HH

Tel: 01786 833635
Fax: 01786 832625

10 bedrooms, 8 with private facilities; Free House; Historic interest; Bar and restaurant meals lunchtime and evenings; Children welcome; Car park; Stirling 3 miles; £££.

The Eagleton Hotel lies close to historic Stirling and the main motorway network; the scenic Trossachs are a short drive away. The attractively furnished bedrooms all have colour television, welcome tea/coffee tray, direct-dial telephone and central heating and most have en suite bath/shower room; two large family rooms are available. The management and staff take particular pride in offering a comprehensive menu, both in the intimate restaurant and in the lounge bar, and a range of beers, wines and spirits, including a wide selection of malt whiskies, is available. Business meetings and social functions can also be catered for. 🌸 🌸 🌸 *Commended.*

Other specialised

FHG PUBLICATIONS

* Recommended SHORT BREAK HOLIDAYS IN BRITAIN   £3.60

* Recommended COUNTRY HOTELS OF BRITAIN   £3.60

* PETS WELCOME!   £3.99

* BED AND BREAKFAST IN BRITAIN   £2.90

Published annually. Please add 50p postage (U.K. only)
when ordering from the publishers:

FHG PUBLICATIONS LTD
Abbey Mill Business Centre, Seedhill,
Paisley, Renfrewshire PA1 1TJ

Are you ready to take the place of her mum?

Leaving mum can be scary for a small puppy. But if you feed Beta Puppy at least the food's as good as mum's was. For details on the full Beta range call the Beta Petcare Advice Service on 0638 552266 or write to PO Box 53, Newmarket, Suffolk CB8 8QF.

BETA ®
petfoods
Food for Life

The Golden Bowl Supplement for Pet-Friendly Pubs

BETA
petfoods

When Beta Petfoods launched its search for Britain's warmest pet welcome, in the form of the Beta Petfoods Golden Bowl Awards Scheme, the response was staggering. Hundreds wrote nominating their pubs for a Golden Bowl award and the chance to be recognisd as kind-hearted publicans for their willingness to provide a bowl of water for their canine customers also.

The pick of the pet pubs (and hotels) have gone into this Supplement to enable owners travelling, holidaying or just walking their dogs to find a warm welcome for *everyone* in the party when they stop for refreshment. We only wish we had room to include more!

BETA PETFOODS has combined sound nutritional expertise with first class innovation to provide a range which has established itself over the last twenty years as a leading brand in complete dog foods, sold nationally through sepcialist outlets, pet shops, vets and country stores.

Particularly renowned for their life cycle feeding programme Beta provide all the necessary nutrients to help keep dogs healthy and fit throughout life. Understanding that every dog is different, Beta has created a range of foods suitable for the demands of all dogs whatever their age and lifestyle: *Beta Puppy* for the vital early growth stage; *Beta Junior* for young, growing dogs; *Beta Recipe* for active pets: *Beta Pet* for less active and older dogs; *Beta Field* for active, working dogs and *Beta Champion* for highly active and breeding dogs.

All manufactured to the highest quality providing excellent palatability and maximum enjoyment.

For further advice on what to feed your pet, please write to: **Spillers Beta Petcare Advice Service, Moulton Road, Kennett, near Newmarket, Suffolk CB8 8QU.**

The Golden Bowl Supplement for Pet-Friendly Pubs

AVON

PRINCE'S MOTTO
Barrow Gurney, near Bristol, Avon.

Dogs allowed in non-food areas and beer garden.

Pet Regulars: Martha (Golden Retriever), serious eating and sleeping.

BERKSHIRE

THE GREYHOUND (known locally as 'The Dog')
The Walk, Eton Wick, Berkshire.

Dogs allowed throughout the pub.

Pet Regulars: Include Lady (GSD), at one o'clock sharp she howls for her hot dog; Trevor (Labrador/Retriever), who does nothing; Skipper (Jack Russell), the local postman's dog and Natasha (GSD) who simply enjoys the ambience.

NOTE
A few abbreviations and 'pet' descriptions have been used in this section which deserve mention and, where necessary, explanation as follows: **GSD:** German Shepherd Dog. **. . . -cross:** a cross-breed where one breed appears identifiable. **57:** richly varied origin. You will also enounter **'mongrel', 'Bitsa' and '???!'** which are self-evident and generally affectionate.

THE QUEEN

Harts Lane, Burghclere, near Newbury, Berkshire.

Dogs allowed throughout the pub.

Pet Regulars: Sam (Border Terrier), makes solo visits to the pub to play with resident long-haired Dachshund Gypsy.

THE SWAN

9 Mill Lane, Clewer, Windsor, Berkshire.

Dogs allowed throughout the pub.

Pet Regulars: Include Luke (Samoyed), enjoys a glass of Tiger beer.

THE TWO BREWERS

Park Street, Windsor, Berkshire.

Dogs allowed, public and saloon bars.

Pet Regulars: Missy and Worthey (Huskies), prefer to remain outside; Sam (Golden Retriever), will retrieve any food and eat it while owner is not looking; Bumble (Highland Terrier), better known as the Highland Hooverer.

BUCKINGHAMSHIRE

WHITE HORSE

Village Lane, Hedgerley, Buckinghamshire SL2 3UY.

Dogs allowed at tables on pub frontage, beer garden (on leads), public bar.

Pet Regulars: Digby (Labrador), the entertainer; Cooper (Boxer), tries hard to better himself – also drinks!

CAMBRIDGESHIRE

YE OLD WHITE HART

Main Street, Ufford, Peterborough.

Dogs allowed in non-food areas.

Pet Regulars: Henry and Robotham (Springer Spaniels), 'pub dog' duties include inspection of all customers and their dogs and, on occasion, seeing them home after last orders.

CHESHIRE

JACKSONS BOAT
Rifle Road, Sale, Cheshire.

Dogs allowed throughout with the exception of the dining area.

Pet Regulars: Bix (Labrador), will share pork scratchings with pub cat, chases beer garden squirrels on solo missions; hamburger scrounging a speciality.

CLEVELAND

TAP AND SPILE
27 Front Street, Framwellgate Moor, Durham DH1 5EE

Dogs allowed throughout the pub except between 12 and 1.30 lunchtimes.

Pet Regulars: These include Smutty (Labrador) who brings her own beer bowl and is definitely *not* a lager Lab – traditional brews only.

CORNWALL

THE WHITE HART
Chilsworthy, near Gunnislake, Cornwall.

Dogs allowed in non-food bar, car park tables, beer garden.

Pet Regulars: Joe (Terrier-cross), sleeps on back under bar stools; Max (Staffordshire-cross) lager drinker; Tatler (Cocker Spaniel), pork cracklings fan; Sheba (GSD), welcoming committee.

CUMBRIA

BRITANNIA INN
Elterwater, Ambleside, Cumbria.

Dogs allowed throughout.

Pet Regulars: Bonnie (sheepdog/Retriever), beer-mat catching, scrounging, has own chair.

THE MORTAL MAN HOTEL
Troutbeck, Windermere, Cumbria LA23 1PL

Dogs allowed throughout and in guest rooms.

Pet Regulars: Include James (Labrador) who will take dogs for walks if they are on a lead and Snip (Border Collie), makes solo visits.

STAG INN
Dufton, Appleby, Cumbria.

Dogs allowed in non-food bar, beer garden, village green.

Pet Regulars: Bachus (Newfoundland), enjoys a good sprawl; Kirk (Dachshund), carries out tour of inspection unaccompanied – but wearing lead; Kim (Weimaraner), best bitter drinker; Buster (Jack Russell), enjoys a quiet evening.

WATERMILL INN
School Lane, Ings, near Staveley, Kendal, Cumbria.

Dogs allowed in beer garden, Wrynose bottom bar.

Pet Regulars: Smudge (sheepdog); Gowan (Westie) and Scruffy (mongrel). All enjoy a range of crisps and snacks. Scruffy regularly drinks Theakstons XB. Pub dogs Misty (Beardie) and Thatcher (Lakeland Terrier).

DERBYSHIRE

DOG AND PARTRIDGE COUNTRY INN & MOTEL
Swinscoe, Ashbourne, Derbyshire.

Dogs allowed throughout, except restaurant.

Pet Regulars: Include Mitsy (57); Rusty (Cairn); Spider (Collie/GSD) and Rex (GSD).

RIFLE VOLUNTEER
Birchwood Lane, Somercotes, Derbyshire DE55 4ND.

Dogs allowed in non-food bar, car park tables, beer garden.

Pet Regulars: Flossy (Border Collie), bar stool inhabitant; Pepper (Border Collie), has made a study of beer mat aerodynamics; Tara (GSD), pub piggyback specialist.

WHITE HART
Station Road, West Hallam, Derbyshire DE7 6GW.

Dogs allowed in all non-food areas.

Pet Regulars: Ben and Oliver (Golden Retrievers), drinking halves of mixed; Sid (Greyhound), plays with cats.

DEVON

BRENDON HOUSE HOTEL
Brendon, Lynton, North Devon EX35 6PS.

Dogs allowed in garden, guest bedrooms.

Pet Regulars: Mutley (mongrel), cat chasing; Pie (Border Terrier), unusual 'yellow stripe', was once chased – by a sheep! Farthing (cat), 20 years old, self appointed cream tea receptionist. Years of practice have perfected dirty looks at visiting dogs.

THE BULLERS ARMS
Chagford, Newton Abbot, Devon.

Dogs allowed throughout pub, except dining room/kitchen.

Pet Regulars: Miffin & Sally (Cavalier King Charles Spaniels), celebrated Miffin's 14th birthday with a party at The Bullers.

CROWN AND SCEPTRE
2 Petitor Road, Torquay, Devon TQ1 4QA.

Dogs allowed in non-food bar, family room, lounge.

Pet Regulars: Samantha (Labrador), opens, consumes and returns empties when offered crisp packets; Toby & Rory (Irish Setters), general daftness; Buddy & Jessie (Collies), beer-mat frisbee experts; Cassie (Collie), scrounging.

THE DEVONSHIRE INN
Sticklepath, near Okehampton, Devon EX20 2NW.

Dogs allowed in non-food bar, car park, beer garden, family room, guest rooms.

Pet Regulars: Bess (Labrador), 'minds' owner; Annie (Shihtzu), snoring a speciality; Daisy (Collie), accompanies folk singers; Duke (GSD) and Ben (Collie-cross), general attention seeking.

THE JOURNEY'S END INN
Ringmore, near Kingsbridge, South Devon TQ7 4HL.

Dogs allowed throughout the pub.

Pet Regulars: Lager, Cider, Scrumpy and Whiskey (all Terriers) – a pint of real ale at lunchtime between them.

THE ROYAL OAK INN

Dunsford, near Exeter, Devon EX6 7DA.

Dogs allowed in non-food bars, beer garden, accommodation for guests with dogs.

Pet Regulars: Tom Thumb (Jack Russell), pub bouncer – doesn't throw people out, just bounces.

THE SEA TROUT INN

Staverton, near Totnes, Devon TQ9 6PA.

Dogs allowed in non-food bar, car park tables, beer garden, owners' rooms (but not on beds).

Pet Regulars: Billy (labrador-cross), partial to drip trays; Curnow (Poodle), brings a blanket.

THE WHITE HART HOTEL

Moretonhampstead, Newton Abbott, Devon TQ13 8NF.

Dogs allowed throughout, except restaurant.

Pet Regulars: Poppie, Rosie (Standard Poodles) and Bobby (Collie).

ESSEX

THE OLD SHIP

Heybridge Basin, Heybridge, Maldon, Essex.

Dogs allowed throughout pub.

Pet Regulars: Toby (57), monopolising bar stools; Tag (Spaniel), nipping behind the bar for biscuits; Toto (57), nipping behind the bar to 'beat up' owners' Great Dane; Happy (terrier), drinking beer and looking miserable.

THE WINGED HORSE

Luncies Road, Vange, Basildon, Essex SS14 1SB.

Dogs allowed throughout pub.

Pet Regulars: Gina (Newfoundland), visits solo daily for a pub lunch – biscuits and a beer; Roxy (Bull Terrier), fond of making a complete mess with crisps and loves a glass of beer. There are 14 canine regulars in all, not including the pub dog Tinka.

THE WOODEN FENDER
Harwich Road, Ardleigh, Essex CO7 7PA.

Dogs allowed in non-food bar, car park tables, beer garden.

Pet Regulars: Holly (Labrador), part-time door stop and vacuum cleaner (paid in marrow-bones); Busty (Labrador), when not eating crisps, thinks/dreams of eating crisps.

GLOUCESTERSHIRE

THE OLD LODGE INN
Minchinhampton Common, Stroud, Gloucestershire GL6 9AQ.

Dogs allowed throughout the pub with the exception of the restaurant.

Pet Regulars: Bess (Labrador) waits nibbling on a carrot while her owners dine in the restaurant; Dotty (Labrador) was a bridesmaid and came to her owner's wedding reception at the pub last year; Katar (Boxer), a fixation with 'chews', distinguished for having won Crufts 'Best Veteran' last year.

GREATER LONDON

THE PHOENIX
28 Thames Street, Sunbury on Thames, Middlesex.

Dogs allowed in non-food bar, beer garden, family room.

Pet Regulars: Pepe (57), fire hog; Cromwell (King Charles), often accompanied by small, balled-up sock. Drinks Websters, once seen with a hangover; Fred (Labrador), would be a fire hog if Pepe wasn't always there first; Oliver (Standard Poodle), still a pup, pub visits are character-building!

THE TIDE END COTTAGE
Ferry Road, Teddington, Middlesex.

Dogs allowed throughout the pub.

Pet Regulars: Angus (Setter), "mine's a half of Guinness"; Dina (GSD), guide dog, beautiful, loyal and clever; Harry (Beagle), partial to sausages, a greeter and meeter; Lady (cross), likes a game of tug o' war with Angus.

143

HAMPSHIRE

THE CHEQUERS
Ridgeway Lane, Lower Pennington, Lymington.

Dogs allowed in non-food bar, outdoor barbecue area (away from food).

Pet Regulars: Otto (Hungarian Vizsla), eats beer-mats and paper napkins. Likes beer but not often indulged.

FLYING BULL
London Road Rake, near Petersfield, Hampshire GU33 7JB.

Dogs allowed throughout the pub.

Pet Regulars: Flippy (Labrador/Old English Sheepdog), partial to the biscuits served with coffee. Status as 'pub dog' questionable as will visit The Sun over the road for a packet of cheese snips.

THE VICTORY
High Street, Hamble-le-Rice, Southampton.

Dogs allowed throughout the pub.

Pet Regulars: Sefton (Labrador), his 'usual' chew bars are kept especially.

HERTFORDSHIRE

THE BLACK HORSE
Chorly Wood Common, Dog Kennel Lane, Rickmansworth, Hertfordshire.

Dogs allowed throughout the pub.

Pet Regulars: Spritzy (mongrel), pub hooligan, former Battersea Dogs' Home resident.

THE FOX
496 Luton Road, Kinsbourne Green, near Harpenden, Hertfordshire.

Dogs allowed in non-food bar, car park tables, beer garden.

Pet Regulars: A tightly knit core of regulars which includes assorted Collies, German Shepherd Dogs and Retrievers. Much competition for dropped bar snacks.

THE ROBIN HOOD AND LITTLE JOHN
Rabley Heath, near Codicote, Hertfordshire.

Dogs allowed in non-food bar, car park tables, beer garden, pitch and putt.

Pet Regulars: Willow (Labrador), beer-mat catcher. The locals of the pub have close to 50 dogs between them, most of which visit from time to time. The team includes a two Labrador search squad dispatched by one regular's wife to indicate time's up. When they arrive he has five minutes' drinking up time before all three leave together.

HUMBERSIDE

BARNES WALLIS INN
North Howden, Howden, North Humberside.

Dogs allowed throughout the pub.

Pet Regulars: A healthy cross-section of mongrels, Collies and Labradors. One of the most popular pastimes is giving the pub cat a bit of a run for his money.

BLACK SWAN
Asselby, Goole, North Humberside.

Dogs allowed in non-food bar.

Pet Regulars: A variety of canine customers.

KINGS HEAD INN
Barmby on the Marsh, North Humberside DN14 7HL.

Dogs allowed in non-food bar.

Pet Regulars: Many and varied!

ISLE OF WIGHT

THE CLARENDON HOTEL AND WIGHT MOUSE INN
Chale, Isle of Wight.

Dogs allowed throughout.

Pet Regulars: Guy (mongrel), calls in for daily sausages. Known to escape from house to visit solo. Hotel dog is Gizmo (Spoodle – Toy Poodle-cross King Charles Spaniel), child entertainer.

KENT

KENTISH HORSE

Cow Lane, Mark Beech, Edenbridge, Kent.

Dogs allowed throughout.

Pet Regulars: Include Boozer (Greyhound), who enjoys a beer and Kylin (Shihtzu), socialising. Pub grounds also permanent residence to goats, sheep, lambs, a horse and geese.

THE OLD NEPTUNE

Marine Terrace, Whitstable, Kent CT5 1EJ.

Dogs allowed in non-food bar and beach frontage.

Pet Regulars: Josh (mongrel), solo visits, serves himself from pub water-bowl; Bear (GSD), insists on people throwing stones on beach to chase, will drop stones on feet as quick reminder; Trigger (mongrel), accompanied by toys; Poppy & Fred (mongrel and GSD), soft touch and dedicated vocalist – barks at anything that runs away!

PRINCE ALBERT

38 High Street, Broadstairs, Kent CT10 1LH.

Dogs allowed in non-food bar.

Pet Regulars: Buster (King Charles), a health freak who likes to nibble on raw carrots and any fresh veg; Suki (Jack Russell), Saturday-night roast beef sampler; Sally (Airdale). official rug; Bruno (Boxer), particularly fond of pepperami sausage.

THE SWANN INN

Little Chart, Kent TN27 0QB.

Dogs allowed – everywhere except restaurant.

Pet Regulars: Rambo (Leonbergers), knocks on the door and orders pork scratchings; Duster (Retriever), places his order – for crisps – with one soft bark for the landlady; Ben (GSD), big licks; Josh (Papillon), hind-legged dancer.

UNCLE TOM'S CABIN

Lavender Hill, Tonbridge, Kent.

Dogs allowed in non-food bar, beer garden.

Pet Regulars: Bob Minor (Lurcher); Tug (mongrel); Bitsy (mongrel); Tilly (Spaniel): 10pm is dog biscuit time!

LANCASHIRE

ABBEYLEE
Abbeyhills Road, Oldham, Lancashire.

Dogs allowed throughout.

Pet Regulars: Include Susie (Boxer), so fond of pork scratchings they are now used by her owners as a reward in the show ring.

MALT'N HOPS
50 Friday Street, Chorley, Lancashire PR6 0AH.

Dogs allowed throughout pub.

Pet Regulars: Freya (German Shepherd Dog), greets everyone by rolling over to allow tummy tickle; Abbie (GSD), under-seat sleeper; Brandy (Rhodesian Ridgeback), at the sound of a bag of crisps opening will lean on eater until guest's legs go numb or offered a share; Toby (Labrador), valued customer in his own right, due to amount of crisps he eats, also retrieves empty bags.

LEICESTERSHIRE

CHEQUERS INN
1 Gilmorton Road, Ashby Magna, near Lutterworth, Leicestershire.

Dogs allowed throughout the pub.

Pet Regulars: Bracken (Labrador), barmaid; Jessie (Labrador), socialite; Blue (English Setter), 'fuss' seeker.

LINCOLNSHIRE

THE BLUE DOG INN
Main Street, Sewstern, Grantham NG33 5QR.

Dogs allowed in non-food bar, beer garden. Dog-hitching rail outside.

Pet Regulars: The Guv'nor (Great Dane), best draught-excluder in history; Jenny (Westie) shares biscuits with pub cats; Jemma (98% Collie), atmosphere lapper-upper, JoJo (Cavalier King Charles), enjoys a drop of Murphys.

MERSEYSIDE

AMBASSADOR PRIVATE HOTEL

13 Bath Street, Southport PR9 0DP.

Dogs allowed in non-food bar, lounge, guest bedrooms.

THE SCOTCH PIPER

Southport Road, Lydiate, Merseyside.

Dogs allowed throughout the pub.

Pet Regulars: Pippa (Rescued Russell), one dog welcoming committee, hearth rug, scrounger. Landlord's dogs very much second fiddle.

MIDLANDS

AWENTSBURY HOTEL

21 Serpentine Road, Selly Park, Birmingham B29 7HU.

Dogs allowed in non-food bar, car park tables, beer garden.

Pet Regulars: Well-behaved dogs welcome.

TALBOT HOTEL

Colley Gate, Halesowen, West Midlands.

Dogs are allowed throughout the pub.

Pet Regulars: Include Inga, Gil, Jack and Red, all Border Collies. Every Christmas canine customers are treated to gift-wrapped dog chews.

NORFOLK

MARINE HOTEL

10 St Edmunds Terrace, Hunstanton, Norfolk PE36 5EH.

Dogs allowed throughout, except dining room.

Pet Regulars: Many dogs have returned with their owners year after year to stay at The Marine Bar.

THE OLD RAILWAY TAVERN

Eccles Road, Quidenham, Norwich, Norfolk NR16 2JG.

Dogs allowed in non-food bar, beer garden.

Pet Regulars: Maggie (Clumber Spaniel); Indi (GSD), Soshie (GSD) and pub dogs Elsa (GSD) & Vell (Springer). Elsa is so fond of sitting, motionless, on her own window ledge; new customers often think she's stuffed!

THE ROSE AND CROWN

Nethergate Street, Harpley, King's Lynn, Norfolk.

Dogs allowed in non-food bar, car park tables, beer garden.

Pet Regulars: A merry bunch with shared interests – Duffy (mongrel); Tammy (Airdale); Bertie & Pru (Standard Poodles) all enjoy pub garden romps during summer and fireside seats in winter.

OXFORDSHIRE

THE BELL INN

High Street, Adderbury, Oxon.

Dogs allowed throughout the pub.

Pet Regulars: Include Wilf (mongrel), supplies full cabaret including talking to people and singing.

SHROPSHIRE

LONGMYND HOTEL

Cunnery Road, Church Stretton, Shropshire SY6 6AG.

Dogs allowed in owners' hotel bedrooms.

Pet Regulars: Sox (Collie/Labrador), occasional drinker and regular customer greeter; Kurt (German Shepherd Dog), entertainments manager; Sadie (Retriever), self appointed fire-guard.

REDFERN HOTEL

Cleobury Mortimer, Shropshire CY14 8AA.

Dogs allowed throughout and guests' bedrooms.

SOMERSET

THE BUTCHERS ARMS

Carhampton, Somerset TA 24

Dogs allowed throughout the pub.

Pet Regulars: Lobo and Chera (Samoyeds), eating ice cubes and drinking; Emma (Spaniel), a whisky drinker; Benji (Spaniel-cross), self-appointed rug. Jimmy, a pony, also occasionally drops in for a drink.

149

HALFWAY HOUSE
Pitney, Langport, Somerset TA10 9AB.

Dogs allowed throughout (except kitchen!).

Pet Regulars: Pip (Lurcher), enjoys bitter, cider and G&T; Bulawayo (Ridgeback-cross), the advance party, sometimes three hours in advance of owner; Potter (57), sits at the bar.

THE SHIP INN
High Street, Porlock, Somerset.

Dogs allowed throughout and in guests' rooms.

Pet Regulars: Include Buster, Hardy and Crackers (Jack Russells), terrorists from London; Bijoux (Peke), while on holiday at The Ship enjoys Chicken Supreme cooked to order every evening.

STAFFORDSHIRE

WATERLOO
Ashby Road, Burton on Trent, Staffordshire.

Dogs allowed throughout pub.

Pet Regulars: They include Tuesday (Collie/German Shepherd), has first claim on a particular corner and won't budge.

SURREY

THE CRICKETERS
12 Oxenden Road, Tongham, Farnham, Surrey.

Dogs allowed in non-food bar, beer garden.

Pet Regulars: Include Lucy (a 'Bitsa'), surreptitious beer drinker and Chocolate Labradors Marston – after the beer – and Tullamore Dew – after the whisky.

WATTENDEN ARMS
Old Lodge Lane, Kenley, Surrey CR2 5RU.

Dogs allowed in non-food bar, beer garden.

Pet Regulars: Freya (GSD), partial to seafood; Karrie (Spaniel), children's entertainer; Ollie (Collie), shakes 'hands' with anyone with a drink; Sam (Springer), likes to fight and run up walls.

SUSSEX

CHARCOAL BURNER
Weald Drive, Furnace Green, Crawley, West Sussex RH10 6NY.

Dogs allowed in non-food bar areas and beer garden.

Pet Regulars: Lucy (Irish Setter), dedicated to cheese snips.

THE FORESTERS ARMS
High Street, Fairwarp, near Uckfield, Sussex TN22 3BP.

Dogs allowed in the beer garden and at car park tables, also inside.

Pet Regulars: Include Scampi (Jack Russell) who enjoys a social interlude with fellow canine guests.

THE INN IN THE PARK (CHEF & BREWER)
Tilgate Park, Tilgate, Crawley, West Sussex RH10 5PQ.

Dogs allowed in non-food bar, beer garden, family room, upstairs lounge and balcony.

Pet Regulars: Tuffy (Staffordshire Bull Terrier) leans, on hind legs, on bar awaiting beer and nibbles; Ted (Weimarawer), a 'watcher'; Jacko (Dalmatian), a crisp howler who, once given a pack, opens them himself; Meg (Border Collie), hoovers fallen bar snacks.

THE PLOUGH
Crowhurst, near Battle, Sussex TN33 9AY.

Dogs allowed in non-food bar, car park tables, beer garden.

Pet Regulars: Kai (Belgian Shepherd), drinks halves of Websters; Poppy and Cassie (Springer Spaniels), divided between the lure of crisps and fireside.

THE PRESTONVILLE ARMS
64 Hamilton Road, Brighton, East Sussex.

Dogs allowed in beer garden, throughout the pub (no food served).

Pet Regulars: These include Katie and Susie, a Yorkie and a ???!, who have been known to jump onto the pool table and help out by picking up the balls.

151

QUEENS HEAD

Village Green, Sedlescombe, East Sussex.

Dogs allowed throughout the pub.

Pet Regulars: Misty (Whippet) partial to Guinness and Bacardi and Coke. Hogs the dog biscuits kept especially for guests' dogs – proceeds to Guide Dogs for the Blind.

THE SLOOP INN

Freshfield Lock, Haywards Heath, Sussex RH17 7NP.

Dogs allowed in non-food bar, at car park tables, beer garden, family room, public bar.

Pet Regulars: Pub dogs are Staffordshire Bull Terriers Rosie and Chutney. Customers include Solo (Labrador), crisp burglar, beer drinker; Tania (Rottweiller), sleeping giant. All bedraggled gun-dogs are especially welcome to dry out by the fire.

THE SMUGGLERS' ROOST

125 Sea Lane, Rustington, West Sussex BN16 25G.

Dogs allowed in non-food bar, at car park tables, beer garden, family room.

Pet Regulars: Moffat (Border Terrier), beer makes him sneeze; Leo (Border Terrier), forms instant affections with anyone who notices him; Max (Cocker Spaniel), eats crisps only if they are 'plain'; Tim (King Charles Spaniel), quite prepared to guard his corner when food appears. The landlord owns a Great Dane.

THE SPORTSMAN'S ARMS

Rackham Road, Amberley, near Arundel BN18 9NR.

Dogs allowed throughout the pub.

Pet Regulars: Ramsden (Labrador), likes pickled onions. Landlord's dogs will not venture into the cellar which is haunted by the ghost of a young girl.

WELLDIGGERS ARMS

Lowheath, Petworth, West Sussex GU28 0HG.

Dogs allowed throughout the pub.

Pet Regulars: Angus (Labrador), crisp snaffler; Benji (Cavalier King Charles), hearth rug.

THE WYNDHAM ARMS
Rogate, West Sussex GU31 5HG.

Dogs allowed in non-food bar, at outside tables and in B&B guest rooms.

Pet Regulars: Henry (wire-haired Dachshund), hooked on Bristol Cream Sherry; Blot (Labrador), welcoming-committee and food fancier; Scruffy (Beardie), completely mad; Oscar (Labrador), floor hog.

WILTSHIRE

ARTICHOKE
The Nursery, Devizes, Wiltshire SN10 2AA.

Dogs allowed throughout pub.

Pet Regulars: Heidi (mongrel), pub tart; Monty (Dalmatian), trifle fixated; Rosie (Boxer), customer 'kissing'; Triffle (Airdale) and Shandy (mongrel) pub welcoming-committee.

THE PETERBOROUGH ARMS
Dauntsey Lock, near Chippenham, Wiltshire SN15 4HD.

Dogs allowed in non-food bar, at car park tables, beer garden, family room (when non-food).

Pet Regulars: Include Winston (Jack Russell), will wait for command before eating a biscuit placed on his nose; Waddi (GSD), can grab a bowling ball before it hits the skittle pins; Harry 4 Legs (GSD), always wins the Christmas prize draw.

THE THREE HORSESHOES
High Street, Chapmanslade, near Westbury, Wiltshire.

Dogs allowed in non-food bar and beer garden.

Pet Regulars: Include Clieo (Golden Retriever), possibly the youngest 'regular' in the land – his first trip to the pub was at eight weeks. Westbury and District Canine Society repair to the Three Horseshoes after training nights (Monday/Wednesday). The pub boasts six cats and two dogs in residence.

WAGGON AND HORSES
High Street, Wootton Bassett, Swindon, Wiltshire.

Dogs allowed in non-food bar.

Pet Regulars: Include Gemma, a very irregular Whippet/Border collie-cross. She likes to balance beer-mats on her nose, then flip them over and catch them, opens and shuts doors on command, walks on her hind legs and returns empty crisp bags. She is limited to one glass of Guinness a night.

YORKSHIRE

THE FORESTERS ARMS
Kilburn, North Yorkshire YO6 4AH.

Dogs allowed throughout, except restaurant.

Pet Regulars: Ebony (Labrador) and Jess (Labrador), eating ice cubes off the bar and protecting customers from getting any heat from the fire.

FOX INN
Roxby Staithes, Whitby, North Yorkshire.

Dogs allowed throughout including guests' bedrooms.

Pet Regulars: B&B guests include Lucy and Mouse (Jack Russell & Dachshund); Mattie & Sally (Spaniels) and Meg and George (Bassetts); Lady (57) and another Lady, also a Heinz 57.

THE GOLDEN FLEECE
Lindley Road, Blackley, near Huddersfield.

Dogs allowed in non-food bar, at outside tables.

Pet Regulars: Ellie & Meara (Rhodesian Ridgebacks), starving dog impressions, animated hearthrugs.

THE GREENE DRAGON INN
Hardraw, Hawes, North Yorkshire DL8 3LZ.

Dogs allowed in non-food bar, at car park tables, beer garden, family room.

154

THE HALL

High Street, Thornton Le Dale, Pickering, North Yorkshire YO18 7RR.

Dogs allowed usually throughout the pub.

Pet Regulars: Include Lucy (Jack Russell), she has her own beer glass at the bar, drinks only Newcastle Brown and Floss (mongrel), partial to Carlsberg.

NEW INN HOTEL

Clapham, near Settle, Yorkshire LA2 8HH.

Dogs allowed in non-food bar, beer garden, family room.

Pet Regulars: Ben (Collie-cross), a model customer.

PREMIER HOTEL

66 Esplanade, South Cliff, Scarborough, Yorkshire YO11 2UZ.

Dogs allowed throughout in non-food areas of hotel.

Pet Regulars: enjoy sharing their owners' rooms at no extra cost. There is a walking service available for pets with disabled owners.

THE SHIP

6 Main Street, Greasbrough, Rotherham S61 4PX.

Dogs allowed throughout the pub.

Pet Regulars: Include Hans (Guide Dog), reverts to puppy behaviour when 'off duty' and Ben (Border Terrier), 'frisks' customers for tit-bits.

SIMONSTONE HALL

Hawes, North Yorkshire DL8 3LY.

Dogs allowed throughout hotel except dining area.

Pet Regulars: account for 2,000 nights per annum. More than 50% of guests are accompanied by their dogs, from Pekes to an Anatolian Shepherd (the size of a small Shetland pony!). Two dogs have stayed, with their owners, on 23 separate occasions.

THE SPINNEY

Forest Rise, Balby, Doncaster, South Yorkshire DN4 9HQ.

Dogs allowed throughout the pub.

Pet Regulars: Shamus (Irish Setter), pub thief. Fair game includes pool balls, beer mats, crisps, beer, coats, hats. Recently jumped 15 feet off pub roof with no ill effect. Yan (Labrador), a dedicated guide dog; Sam (Boxer), black pudding devotee.

THE ROCKINGHAM ARMS

8 Main Street, Wentworth, Roherham, South Yorkshire S62 7LO.

Dogs allowed throughout pub.

Pet Regulars: Tilly (Beardie), does nothing but has adopted the quote of actor Kenneth Williams – "Sometimes I feel so unutterably superior to those around me that I marvel at my ability to live among them"; Sasha & Penny (Terriers), enjoy a social coffee; Kate & Rags (Airdale and cross-breed), prefer lager to coffee; Holly (terrier and pub dog), dubbed 'the flying squirrel', likes everyone, whether they like it or not!

ROTHERHAM COMPANIONS CLUB

The Fairways, Wickersley, Rotherham, South Yorkshire.

Dogs allowed throughout the pub (some restrictions if wedding party booked).

Pet Regulars: All chocolate fanatics who receive their favourite treat on arrival include Viking (Springer), Duke (Chow), Max (Border Collie) and Willie (Yorkshire Terrier). Viking keeps a box of toys and a ball behind the bar.

WALES

ANGLESEY

THE BUCKLEY HOTEL

Castle Street, Beaumaris, Isle of Anglesey LL58 8AW.

Dogs allowed throughout the pub, except in the dining room.

Pet Regulars: Cassie (Springer Spaniel) and Rex (mongrel), dedicated 'companion' dogs.

DYFED

THE ANGEL HOTEL

Rhosmaen Street, Lalndeilo, Dyfed.

Dogs allowed throughout the pub.

Pet Regulars: Skip (Spaniel/Collie), a Baileys devotee; Crumble (GSD) a devotee of anything edible.

SCOTLAND

ABERDEENSHIRE

BULL AND TERRIER BAR

Huntly Hotel, 18 The Square, Huntly, Aberdeenshire AB54 5BR.

Dogs allowed in non-food bar, beer garden, family room, guests' rooms.

Pet Regulars: Manni (English Bull Terrier), likes to have his tummy tickled by lady customers; Samantha (Rottweiller), eyes never leave the biscuit barrel; Megan (57), chasing Manni. Manni is also the local football team mascot.

ARGYLL

THE BALLACHULISH HOTEL

Ballachulish, Argyll PA39 4JY.

Dogs allowed in the lounge, beer garden and guests' bedrooms.

Pet Regulars: Thumper (Border Collie/GSD-cross), devoted to his owner and follows him everywhere.

DUMFRIES & GALLOWAY

CULGRUFF HOUSE HOTEL

Crossmichael, Castle Douglas, Dumfries & Galloway DG7 3BB.

Dogs allowed at car park tables, family room, guest bedrooms.

Pet Regulars: A cross section of canine visitors.

MORAYSHIRE

THE CLIFTON BAR

Clifton Road, Lossiemouth, Morayshire.

Dogs allowed throughout pub.

Pet Regulars: Include Zoe (Westie), has her own seat and is served coffee with two lumps and Rhona (Labrador) who makes solo visits.

ROYAL OAK

Station Road, Urquhart, Elgin, Moray.

Dogs allowed throughout pub.

Pet Regulars: Murphy (Staffordshire Bull Terrier) – food bin. Biscuits (from the landlady), Maltesers (from the landlord), sausages and burgers (from the barbecue).

PERTHSHIRE

CLACHAN COTTAGE HOTEL

Lochside, Lochearnhead, Perthshire, Scotland.

Dogs allowed in all non-food areas.

Pet Regulars: Regulars are few but passing trade frequent and welcome. Previous owner's dog was a renowned water-skier.

CHANNEL ISLANDS   *JERSEY*

LA PULENTE INN

La Pulente, St Brelade, Jersey.

Dogs allowed throughout the pub.

Pet Regulars: Include Bridie (Border Collie), darts, pool, watching TV, beer-mat skiing, stone shoving. Also responsible for fly catching. Drinks Bass and Guinness.

158

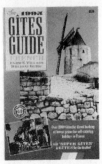

ONE FOR YOUR FRIEND 1995

FHG Publications have a large range of attractive holiday accommodation guides for all kinds of holiday opportunities throughout Britain. They also make useful gifts at any time of year. Our guides are available in most bookshops and larger newsagents but we will be happy to post you a copy direct if you have any difficulty. We will also post abroad but have to charge separately for post or freight. The inclusive cost of posting and packing the guides to you or your friends in the UK is as follows:

**Farm Holiday Guide
ENGLAND, WALES and IRELAND**
Board, Self-catering, Caravans/Camping,
Activity Holidays. Over 400 pages.   **£4.80**

Farm Holiday Guide SCOTLAND
All kinds of holiday accommodation.   **£3.00**

**SELF-CATERING & FURNISHED
HOLIDAYS**
Over 1000 addresses throughout for
Self-catering and caravans in Britain.   **£4.20**

BRITAIN'S BEST HOLIDAYS
A quick-reference general guide
for all kinds of holidays.   **£3.30**

**The FHG Guide to CARAVAN &
CAMPING HOLIDAYS**
Caravans for hire, sites and
holiday parks and centres.   **£3.30**

BED AND BREAKFAST STOPS
Over 1000 friendly and comfortable
overnight stops. Non-smoking, The
Disabled and Special Diets
Supplements.   **£4.40**

**CHILDREN WELCOME! FAMILY
HOLIDAY GUIDE**
Family holidays with details of
amenities for children and babies.   **£4.40**

**Recommended SHORT BREAK
HOLIDAYS IN BRITAIN**
'Approved' accommodation for
quality bargain breaks. Introduced by
John Carter.   **£4.20**

**Recommended COUNTRY HOTELS
OF BRITAIN**
Including Country Houses, for
the discriminating.   **£4.20**

**Recommended WAYSIDE INNS
OF BRITAIN**
Pubs, Inns and small hotels.   **£4.20**

**PGA GOLF GUIDE
Where to play and where to stay**
Over 2000 golf courses in Britain with
convenient accommodation. Endorsed
by the PGA. Holiday Golf in France,
Portugal, Spain and USA.   **£9.50**

PETS WELCOME!
The unique guide for holidays for
pet owners and their pets.   **£4.60**

BED AND BREAKFAST IN BRITAIN
Over 1000 choices for touring and
holidays throughout Britain.
Airports and Ferries Supplement.   **£3.30**

**THE FRENCH FARM AND VILLAGE
HOLIDAY GUIDE**
The official guide to self-catering
holidays in the 'Gîtes de France'.   **£9.50**

Tick your choice and send your order and payment to FHG PUBLICATIONS, ABBEY MILL BUSINESS CENTRE, SEEDHILL, PAISLEY PA1 1TJ (TEL: 0141-887 0428. FAX: 0141-889 7204). **Deduct** 10% for 2/3 titles or copies; 20% for 4 or more.

Send to: NAME ....

ADDRESS ....

....

.... POST CODE ....

I enclose Cheque/Postal Order for £ ....

SIGNATURE .... DATE ....

Please complete the following to help us improve the service we provide. How did you find out about our guides:

☐ Press   ☐ Magazines   ☐ TV   ☐ Radio   ☐ Family/Friend   ☐ Other.

MAP
SECTION

The following seven pages of maps indicate the main
cities, towns and holiday centres of Britain. Space
obviously does not permit every location featured in
this book to be included but the approximate position
may be ascertained by using the distance indications
quoted and the scale bars on the maps.

Map 1

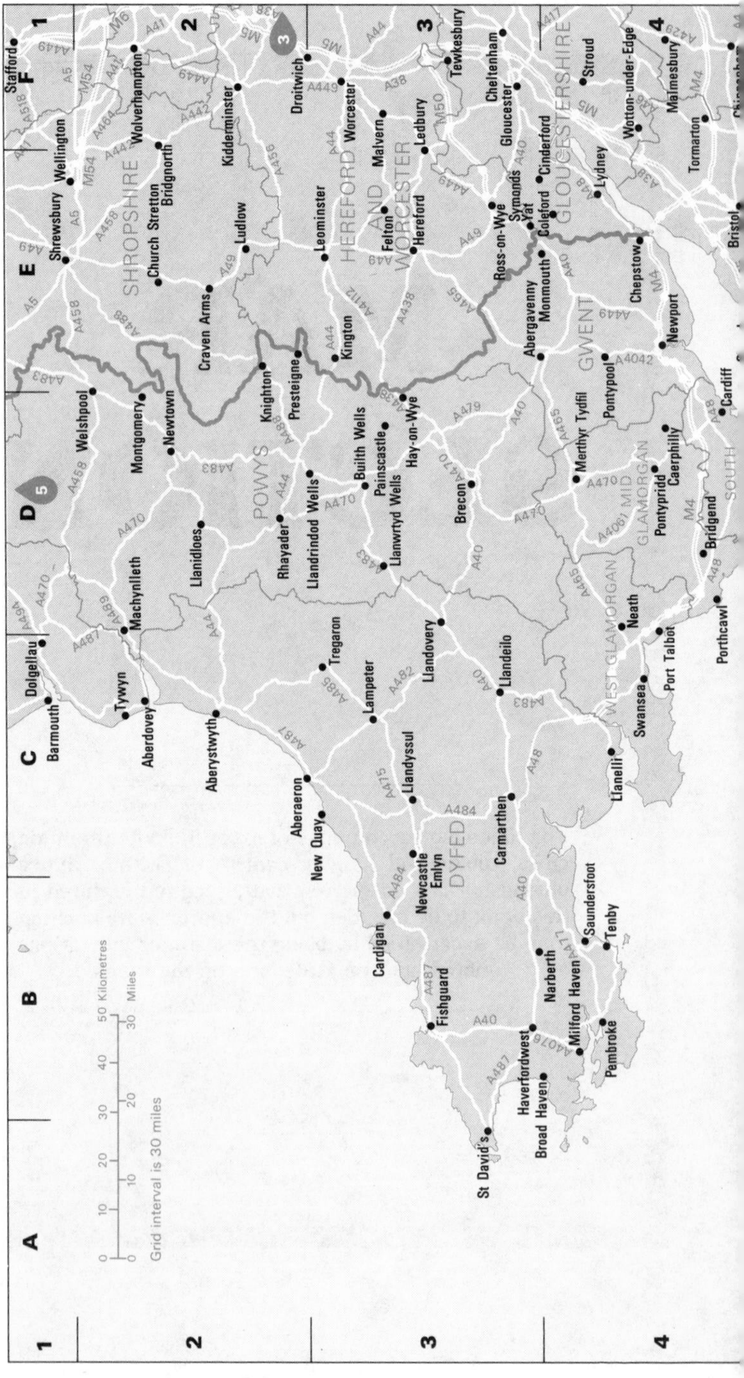

A
B
C
D
E
F
1
2
3
4
Stafford
Wellington
Wolverhampton
Shrewsbury
Bridgnorth
Church Stretton
Kidderminster
Droitwich
Worcester
Malvern
Ledbury
Tewkesbury
Cheltenham
Gloucester
Stroud
Wotton-under-Edge
Malmesbury
Tormarton
Lydney
Cinderford
Symonds Yat
Coleford
Ross-on-Wye
Hereford
Felton
Leominster
Ludlow
Craven Arms
Kington
Presteigne
Knighton
Welshpool
Montgomery
Newtown
Llanidloes
Rhayader
Llandrindod Wells
Builth Wells
Painscastle
Hay-on-Wye
Llanwrtyd Wells
Brecon
Abergavenny
Monmouth
Chepstow
Newport
Pontypool
Merthyr Tydfil
Caerphilly
Cardiff
Pontypridd
Bridgend
Porthcawl
Neath
Port Talbot
Swansea
Llanelli
Llandovery
Llandeilo
Tregaron
Lampeter
Machynlleth
Dolgellau
Barmouth
Tywyn
Aberdovey
Aberystwyth
Aberaeron
New Quay
Llandyssul
Carmarthen
Newcastle Emlyn
Cardigan
Fishguard
Saundersfoot
Tenby
Narberth
Milford Haven
Haverfordwest
Pembroke
Broad Haven
St David's
Bristol
SHROPSHIRE
HEREFORD AND WORCESTER
GLOUCESTERSHIRE
POWYS
GWENT
MID GLAMORGAN
WEST GLAMORGAN
SOUTH
DYFED
Grid interval is 30 miles
0 10 20 30 40 50 Kilometres
10 20 30 Miles

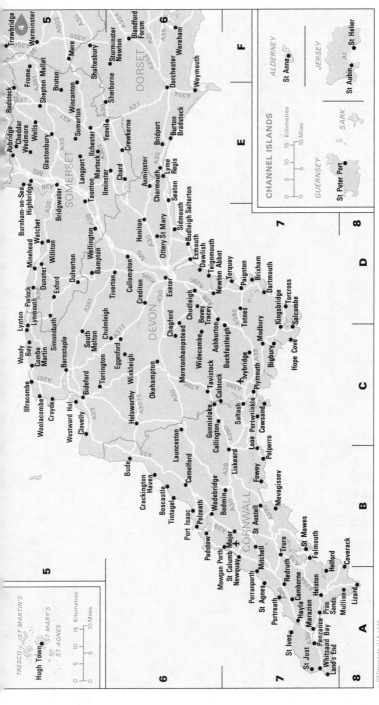

Map 2

© GEOprojects (U.K.) Ltd
Crown Copyright Reserved

Map 3

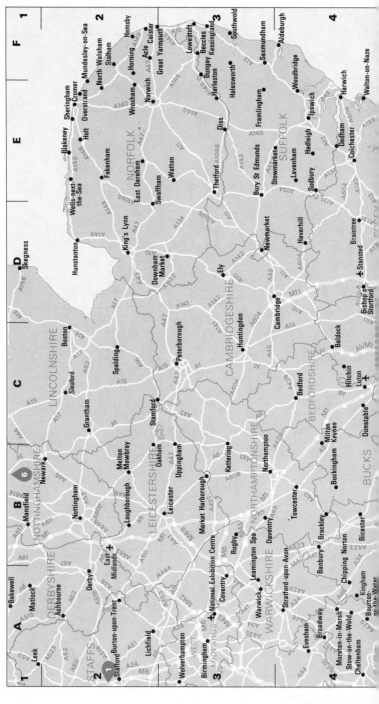

Map 4

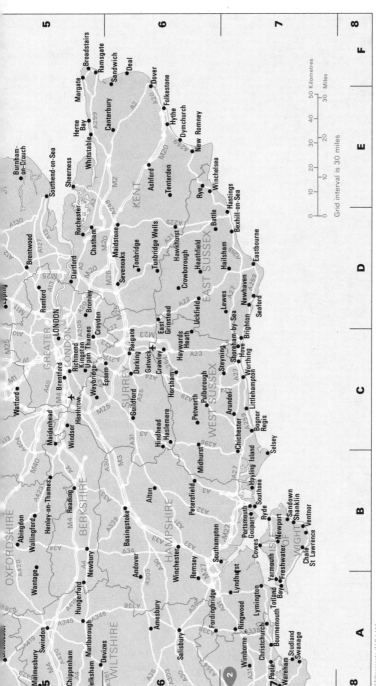

© GEOprojects (U.K.) Ltd
Crown Copyright. Reserved

Grid interval is 30 miles

Miles
Kilometres

A B C D E F

5 6 7 8

Map 5

1 A   B   C 7   D

Girvan

DUMFRIES AND GALLOWAY   Langholm

New Galloway   Belling
NORT

Newton
Stewart   Dumfries   Annan Gretna Longtown
                                    Greenhead
Castle Douglas
Gatehouse of Fleet   Brampton A69
Wigtown   Carlisle
Kirkcudbright   Silloth

Port William   Wigton   Alston

                        Maryport
                        Cockermouth   Bassenthwaite   Penrith
Workington   Keswick   Brampto

Whitehaven   Ennerdale Ullswater Shap   Appleby
             Bridge   CUMBRIA   Kirkby
                                              Stephen
                Gosforth Little Langdale Ambleside
                Seascale   Hawkshead   Windermere
                        Coniston   A685
Ramsey   Newby   Kendal   Sedbergh
Peel   Broughton-in-Furness Bridge
                                          Kirkby Lonsda
Port   ISLE OF MAN   Millom   Ulverston   Ingle
Erin Castletown   Grange-over-Sands
Douglas   Sett
Port St Mary   Barrow-in-Furness
                        Morecambe
                        Lancaster

                        Fleetwood
                                          Clitheroe

                        Blackpool   LANCASHIRE
                        Lytham St Annes   Preston   Blackbu
                                          Chorley
                        Southport   Bolto
                        Formby   Wigan   GREATER
                                          MANCHEST
Amlwch   Hoylake Liverpool MERSEYSIDE Manche
ANGLESEY   Birkenhead   M62
Holyhead Llanerchymedd Llandudno Colwyn Prestatyn
        Menai Beaumaris Bay   Rhyl   Knutsford
Llangefni Bridge Conwy Abergele   Chester Northwich CHESHIRE
        Bangor   Denbigh
Caernarvon Llanrwst   Ruthin   Nantwich
Llanberis Betws-y-Coed   CLWYD   Newcastle-under-L
GWYNEDD   Corwen Wrexham
Nefyn Portmadoc Ffestiniog Bala Llangollen   Market
Criccieth Penrhyndeudraeth   Wem   Drayton
Pwllheli   Oswestry   Wellington
Llanbedrog Harlech   SHROPSHIRE
Aberdaron Abersoch   M54
        Dolgellau   Welshpool
Barmouth   Shrewsbury
                        POWYS
Tywyn Machynlleth

© GEOprojects (U.K.) Ltd
Crown Copyright Reserved

Map 6

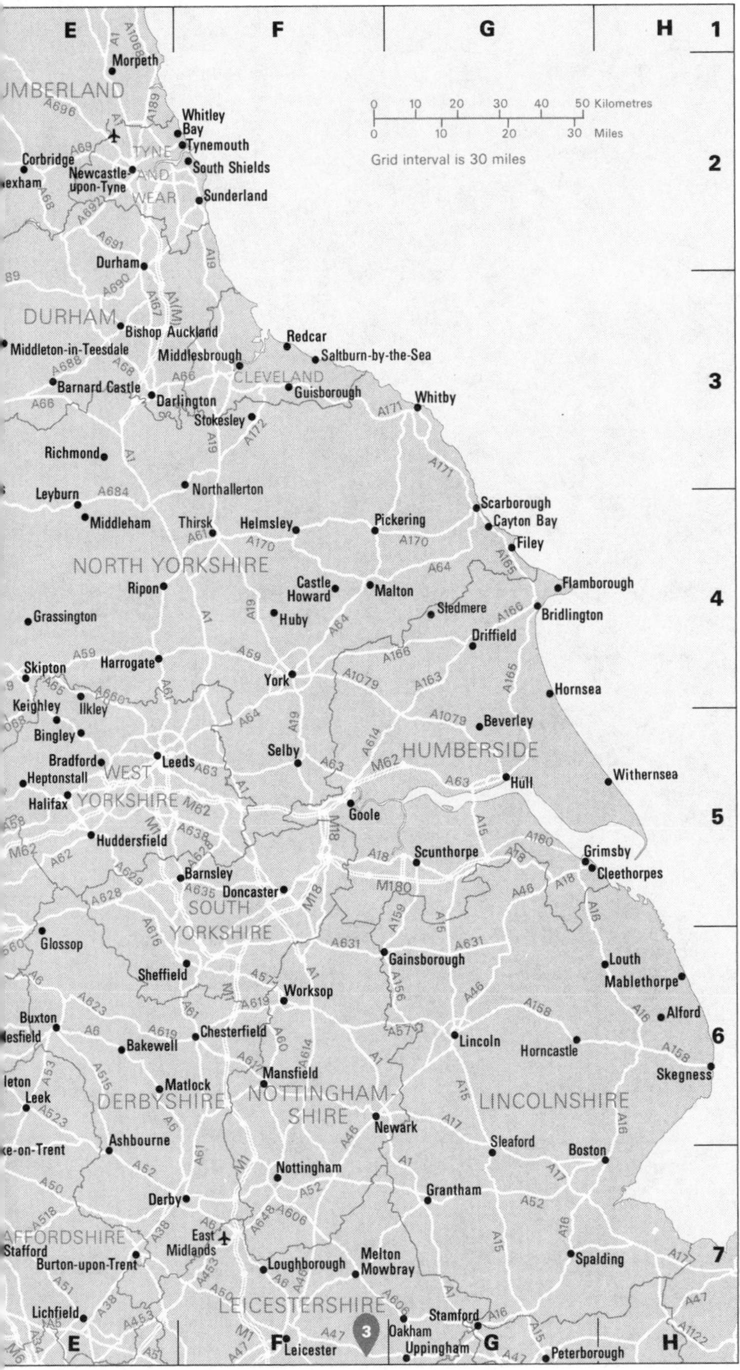

E F G H 1

Morpeth
UMBERLAND
Whitley Bay
Tynemouth
Corbridge
Newcastle upon-Tyne
South Shields
Hexham
TYNE AND WEAR
Sunderland
2

Durham
DURHAM
Bishop Auckland
Redcar
Middleton-in-Teesdale
Middlesbrough
Saltburn-by-the-Sea
Barnard Castle
CLEVELAND
Darlington
Guisborough
Whitby
Stokesley
3

Richmond
Leyburn
Northallerton
Middleham
Thirsk
Helmsley
Pickering
Scarborough
Cayton Bay
Filey
NORTH YORKSHIRE
Ripon
Castle Howard
Malton
Flamborough
Grassington
Huby
Stedmere
Bridlington
Driffield
4

Skipton
Harrogate
York
Hornsea
Keighley
Ilkley
Bingley
Selby
Beverley
Bradford
Leeds
HUMBERSIDE
Heptonstall
WEST YORKSHIRE
Hull
Withernsea
Halifax
Huddersfield
Goole
5

Grimsby
Barnsley
Scunthorpe
Cleethorpes
Glossop
Doncaster
SOUTH YORKSHIRE
Louth
Sheffield
Gainsborough
Mablethorpe
Buxton
Worksop
Alford
Macclesfield
Chesterfield
Lincoln
Horncastle
Bakewell
Skegness
6

Leek
Matlock
Mansfield
LINCOLNSHIRE
DERBYSHIRE
NOTTINGHAM-SHIRE
Newark
Stoke-on-Trent
Ashbourne
Sleaford
Boston
Nottingham
Grantham
Derby
East Midlands
STAFFORDSHIRE
Spalding
Stafford
Burton-upon-Trent
Loughborough
Melton Mowbray
7

Lichfield
LEICESTERSHIRE
Stamford
Oakham
Peterborough
Leicester
Uppingham

E F G H

0 10 20 30 40 50 Kilometres
0 10 20 30 Miles
Grid interval is 30 miles

Map 7

0 10 20 30 40 50 Kilometres
0 10 20 30 Miles
Grid interval is 30 miles

A B C D E F
1 2 3

SHETLAND ISLANDS

YELL

MAINLAND

Lerwick

Sumburgh

ORKNEY MAINLAND
Stromness
Kirkwall
HOY

WESTERN ISLES
LEWIS

Durness
Bettyhill
Tongue
Thurso
John o'Groats
Wick

Scourie
Lochinver
Lairg
Golspie
Helmsdale

Ullapool
Bonar Bridge
Dornoch

Gairloch
Poolewe
Tain

Dingwall
Rosemarkie
Elgin
Cullen
Banff
Fraserburgh

HIGHLAND
Fortrose
Nairn
Forres
Fochabers
Keith
Turriff
Peterhead

Portree
SKYE
RAASAY
Beauly
Inverness
Daviot
Grantown-on-Spey
Huntly
Banff

Kyle of Lochalsh
Dornie
Carrbridge
Tomintoul
Inverurie

Broadford
Kyleakin
Aviemore
GRAMPIAN
Aberdeen

Mallaig
Fort Augustus
Kingussie
Banchory
Stonehaven

HEBRIDES
INNER
Braemar

Fort William
Kinlochleven
Glencoe
Kinloch Rannoch
Pitlochry
Brechin

Ballachulish
Aberfeldy
TAYSIDE
Forfar
Montrose

Tobermory
MULL
Oban
Taynuilt
Killin
Dunkeld
Blairgowrie
Dundee
Arbroath
Carnoustie
Monifieth

Dalmally
Crianlarich
Lochearnhead
Perth
St Andrews

Inveraray
Crieff
Cupar
FIFE

Arrochar
Tarbet
Callander
Auchterarder

JURA
Lochgilphead
Luss
Aberfoyle
Drymen
Kinross
Dunfermline
Kirkcaldy
North Berwick

Ardrishaig
Dunoon
Gourock
Balloch
Dumbarton
CENTRAL
Stirling
EDINBURGH
Dalkeith
Haddington
Dunbar

Tarbert
Greenock
Paisley
Glasgow
LOTHIAN
Eyemouth

ISLAY
Rothesay
Largs
Hamilton
Chirnside
Duns
Berwick upon Tweed

STRATHCLYDE
Ardrossan
Irvine
Kilmarnock
Lanark
Biggar
Lauder
Coldstream
Cornhill-on-Tweed
Barn

Brodick
Troon
Peebles
Galashiels
Kelso
Wooler
Seal

KINTYRE
Lamlash
Prestwick
Ayr
New Cumnock
Abington
Selkirk
Jedburgh
Alnwick

Campbeltown
ARRAN
Maybole
Hawick
BORDERS

Girvan
Moffat
Beattock
NORTHUMBER-LAND

Langholm
Bellingham
Mo

DUMFRIES & GALLOWAY
Newton Stewart
New Galloway
Castle Douglas
Dumfries
Gretna
Longtown
Greenhead
Newcastle-upon-Tyne
Whit
B

Stranraer
Wigtown
Gatehouse of Fleet
Annan
Carlisle
Hexham
Corbridge

Portpatrick
Kirkcudbright
Silloth
CUMBRIA
Alston
F
Durham
G

Port William
Bassenthwaite
Penrith

5 6

© GEOprojects (U.K.) Ltd
Crown Copyright Reserved